Faith Journey:
A Pathway for Traveling with Christ

An Adult Spiritual Formation Process

W. Douglas Hood, Jr.

Foreword by Thomas G. Long

Faith Journey
A Pathway for Traveling with Christ
by W. Douglas Hood, Jr.

Printed in the United States of America

ISBN 9781613790472

www.xulonpress.com

Foreword by Thomas G. Long

In this helpful resource, *FaithJourney: A Pathway for Traveling with Christ*, W. Douglas Hood Jr. not only provides practical guidance for Christians who desire a deeper faith life, he also participates in two significant trends in 21st century American church life.

The first trend reflected in these pages has to do with a creative pastoral response to what has been called the "secularization" of American religious life. It has been widely reported that membership and attendance figures for the old "mainline" denominations in the U.S. have declined precipitously in the last fifty years and that many people in our society today are either uninterested in religion altogether or prefer a non-churchy, "spiritual but not religious" version of it. What has perhaps received less attention is the fact that in many of the congregations that are still strong, maybe even growing, the worshippers are nevertheless affected by secularization. Even though they are still church goers, they are less formed by and informed about the Christian faith than were their great-grandparents. There are now many people who worship regularly in Christian churches, who are eager to be faithful, but who do not have a deep working knowledge of the faith. They desire a richer biblical knowledge, a keener awareness of the basic truth claims of Christianity, and a more profound acquaintance with the practical side of the faith.

Good pastors are recognizing that the task for forming people in faith has a new urgency in our time. Preaching to people who are not learning about the faith and being formed in discipleship can devolve into entertaining an audience instead of edifying a congregation of the faithful. In this book, Doug Hood provides welcome help in this important ministry of weaving into the fabric of people's lives the basic pattern of the Christian faith.

The second trend reflected in this book is the renewed awareness of the importance of practices in the lives of Christians. For too long, we have tended to present the Christian faith as if it were a "head experience" alone, a set of ideas and beliefs to which people said yes or no. But Christianity is not merely a collection of thought and doctrines; it is rather an all-encompassing way of life. Over the centuries, Christians have learned how to shape that way of life by investing their energies in certain spiritually sustaining and life-giving practices, such as reading Scripture together, prayer, service to others, and stewarding resources. Without a clear and structured pattern of practices, the Christian life can be fragmented, shapeless, and incoherent. In this book, Doug Hood helps Christians reclaim these ancient practices in ways that are pertinent in our day.

Doug Hood has written a wise and worthy guide for pastors and lay people. It is the fruit of much study, thought, and prayer, and we are in his debt.

Thomas G. Long
Bandy Professor of Preaching
Candler School of Theology
Emory University
Atlanta, GA

CONTENTS

APPRECIATION

A journey of faith is always made in community: in the company of the Triune God and in the company of others who are on the road with us. Some may have traveled ahead of us but leave behind their wisdom as markers for our journey. Others travel with us, contributing their insights, learnings and glimpses of God as we share ours. Still others are behind us with a careful eye on the horizon for the markers we will leave for them. Together, we all journey into the embrace of our savior, Jesus Christ.

The preparation of this resource has been a special journey for me. The hours of reading, reflection, prayer, writing, and rewriting seem now as numerous as the stars of the night sky. What I am certain of is that, if there is any value here, it is the result of my standing under the wisdom and instruction of many great leaders of the faith – some I have enjoyed in the classroom, others from the printed page. My hope is that something of the force of their insight and guidance in Christian spiritual formation has been captured in these pages.

Perhaps most importantly, this work has been brought to completion because of special companions who have surrounded me, nurtured me, and encouraged me to finish the race when I became weary. Clearly, I would not have been successful without the full support of the following people who, for reasons perhaps know only to them, just keep on believing in me and encouraging me in our shared journey of faith:

The membership of the Lenape Valley Presbyterian Church, New Britain, Pennsylvania, who has invited me the past eleven years to be their pastor and a pilgrim with them in spiritual growth. They have loved my family and me, received my ministry with joy, encouraged me in my own journey of faith, and provided for my family's material needs. They have made ministry among them a place of delight.

Mark Beard, Kurt Pleim, and Peter Thompson, each of you have sustained me in the practice of ministry by your prayers, mutual study of discipleship with me and, most importantly, your special friendship. My time with you provided the inspiration for the development of this resource. Your companionship on the journey has been a treasure.

James W. Bauerle, Bert Schillo, and Stephan K. Hess participated with me in the testing of this material within a Faith Journey Group and provided immeasurable insight for strengthening its usefulness to others. My ministry is the richer for each of you.

Bill Kerber, a colleague in ministry and friend whose imagination and creativity expand my own and who has encouraged me in making this resource available to a wider audience.

Laura Cooney, as always, was a tremendous support with her administrative assistance and help in protecting my preparation time for this project. More, she has been a trusted friend and partner in ministry, whose wise and trusted counsel has strengthened my ministry.

My brother Wayne Hood, along with his wife, Nancy and daughter, Christina never cease praying for me and encouraging me. Most importantly, Wayne's commitment to the local church as a pastor encourages my own.

Jonathan Cameron, my brother-in-law and his wife, Janet, Elisabeth Cameron, my sister-in-law, and Wilma Cameron, my mother-in-law have each made extraordinary sacrifices to support me in the completion of my studies at Fuller Theological Seminary, Pasadena, CA. Additionally, they have contributed to the continued wholeness of my family that has made this work possible.

Most importantly, I deeply appreciate my family, my wife, Grace, and children, Nathanael and Rachael, who gave-up time with me that I may commit energy and time to bring this book to completion. Grace, you are a woman who embodies Christlike character. The Lord's truths, wisdom, and immeasurable love and encouragement always come through you. Thank you for your patience and support for standing with me through the completion of this long project. You, along with two incredible children, have made our life together a joyful place.

Introducing the 14-Week Journey:

Read Before You Begin

The great Scottish preacher and teacher, Peter Taylor Forsyth (1848-1921) once said that there is but one great preacher in history and that preacher is the Church.[1] The first business of the individual preacher, contends Forsyth, is to enable the Church to preach, but it is the Church, the community of faith, which is to declare the message of Christ to the world. The preaching Forsyth speaks of has less to do with the spoken word and more to do with changed lives, "either in direction or in scale."[2] In true preaching, more is done than said. Any other kind of preaching may be interesting but will remain powerless. The gospel of Jesus Christ is not about the enlightenment of minds but the transformation of women and men into the character of Christ.

Unfortunately, as Thomas Long observes in the foreword, many in the church today are less formed by and informed about the Christian faith than were their great-grandparents. The result is exhausted Christians, busy with good and worthy church activities, who have little sense of an intimate relationship with the One whom all their activity is about. Absent is a sense of awe, wonder, and experience of an unnatural power. Membership in the church is just one more activity in an overburdened life. A matter of great urgency before the Church today is identifying a pathway for ordinary people to become moved by the power of God that results in fully devoted followers of Jesus Christ.

The purpose of this resource is to equip the Church for its preaching to the world, to provide a pathway for a purposeful and life changing walk with Jesus Christ. The Christian spiritual formation process identified here will provide clarity on the nature of discipleship, identify five irreducible faith practices for growing in Christ, and guide the development of a personal growth plan. The intention is to offer direction in spiritual formation and accelerate personal spiritual growth. Participants will not only discover their footing on a pathway toward Christlikeness

---

[1] P. T. Forsyth, *Positive Preaching and the Modern Mind* (London: Independent Press, 1953), 53.

[2] Ibid., 54.

but will be introduced to a simple, yet effective means of becoming a self-reproducing disciple of Jesus Christ.

The eight sessions of this study guide will dispel the myth that discipleship is hard work and limited to a few. What will be discovered is that becoming a holy people who are continually being fashioned into the image of Christ is the hard work of the Holy Spirit. What is required of us is that we grant the Holy Spirit access to our lives by becoming imitators of Jesus' life.

Think of it this way. Plant a seed in the ground. It is not our work to cause the seed to sprout and grow. That is a process beyond our power and ability. It is an organic process hard wired into the seed by God. But we do have to plant the seed in good, rich soil. Spiritual growth is much the same. Growth in Christ is as organic as the growth of the seed. But good, rich soil is required. Preparing the soil of our lives simply means that we will follow the practices of Jesus during his life here on earth. It also means that we avoid poisoning the soil with unhealthy practices. As we become imitators of Jesus, the work of transformation into the likeness of Jesus is a natural, organic one. It is the work of the Holy Spirit.

Five Faith Practices

The Church has always recognized that the Christian life has much more to do with our lives than with a mental consent to a collection of thought and beliefs. The Christian life is a call to a reorientation of how we are to live. The emphasis, therefore, is not on conformity of thought but on conformity of action – the imitation of the life of Jesus. Faith practices are a means by which we begin to imitate Jesus, his life and ministry, and consequently give ourselves over to the Holy Spirit in such a manner that we see the image of God increase in our heart. Certain practices carefully identified and incorporated into our way of being and living provide attentiveness to the work of God in our communities and the world. The five, irreducible faith practices identified for this spiritual formation process are:

- Worship Regularly
- Pray Daily
- Learn & Apply God's Word
- Participate in a Ministry
- Give Financially to the Work of the Church.

These practices are what we do, the responsibility we take for our growth. They give evidence of a decision to live differently; the refusal to be conformed to this world but, rather, to be transformed by a life that follows the example of Christ. During the eighth session of this spiritual formation small group process, participants will identify both present strengths and opportunities for growth in the five faith practices using a simple assessment instrument. Guidance will then be provided for developing a personal growth plan for the one or two faith practices that require the most growth.

Basic Formula for Transformation

This spiritual formation process recognizes that spiritual growth does not happen by individual effort alone. Though our active participation in growth is important, little would be accomplished apart from the active work of God in us through the Holy Spirit. What is required is that we place ourselves before God in such a manner that God might accomplish God's work in us. Three opportunities or "places of engagement in spiritual growth" have been identified for this as a basic formula for transformation:

- A Place Alone with God in Silence & Solitude
- A Place in a Community of a Small Group for Encouragement & Accountability
- A Place for Sharing Your Growth with Another.

In these places, we encounter the risen Christ much the same as the disciples did following his resurrection. It is in these places that we experience in our lives the animating power of God that produces change into Christlikeness.

Before looking at the format of the small group sessions, a closer examination of this basic formula for transformation may be helpful.

A Place Alone

Spiritual formation and growth require a growing attentiveness to God, to where God is active in our lives, and to where we are being led. This attentiveness requires that we make a place in our lives to sense God's presence and to hear God speak. Psalm 46:10 teaches that such a place is one of stillness – a place apart from the noise, pace, and narrative of the surrounding culture in which we spend most of our lives. God's narrative, God's desire, God's calling is opened to us in places of silence and solitude. It will be in such places that we permit God to have God's way with us, a place where we experience accelerated growth in spiritual living. Time in such places also builds resistance to all other voices that compete with God's voice in our lives.

A Place in Community

The Kingdom of God is relational. A decision to follow Jesus and grow in his likeness cannot be accomplished alone. The Apostle Paul teaches in his letter to the Roman Church that, though discipleship to the Lordship of Jesus is intensely personal, it is corporate in character (Romans 12:3-5). Matthew's Gospel further asserts that the Church, the community of faith, is the primary means by which God answers the Church's prayer, "Your kingdom come. Your will be done, on earth as it is in heaven" (Matthew 6:10 NRSV). And Ephesians teaches that it is participation in the work of the Church that believers grow into full maturity in Christ (Ephesians 4:13). A call to follow Christ, to be his disciple and exercise spiritual living in the manner of Christ is a clear summons to participate in his community, the Church.

A Place for Sharing

Our daily conversations do more than provide a running narrative of our lives; such conversations shape our experiences, practices and life with one another. The Bible teaches that, as we think, so we become. As we speak, we provide clarity and development of those thoughts that ultimately shape who we will be. The essence of spiritual formation is the quality of life that we live. That life develops positively in the manner of Jesus as our lips take on truthful, meaningful, and compassionate speech that is ultimately grounded in a compelling witness to the place Jesus occupies in our hearts.

There is a marvelous story in the ninth chapter of John's Gospel. A man who was blind was brought to Jesus and received his sight. He went into town to share the miracle of his physical healing. Religious leaders pressed him for a theological assessment of what had occurred. His answer was simple: "One thing I do know, that though I was blind, now I see" (John 9:25 NRSV). He doesn't become captive to their desire for theological debate. Simply, he states his former condition (blindness), and his present condition (sight) as a result of Jesus. When Christians are asked why they do not share their faith more often, the primary reason stated is that they feel inadequate in presenting the Christian faith or fear theological debates they are ill equipped for. The man in John's Gospel gives us permission to sidestep these conversations. Simply share, as he shared, that once I was this way, this is what happened, and now I am another way. Three powerful talking points for sharing:

- **This is where my faith was.**
  Example: Though I always believed in God, my faith lacked depth, structure, and impact upon my life.

- **This is what I did.**
  Example: I joined a spiritual formation process with three other men called *Faith Journey*. Together we studied Scripture, prayed, and held one another accountable for the engagement of certain faith practices in our daily lives.

- **This is where my faith is now.**
  Example: I have grown more assured of God's love for me, cherish new friendships made, and now am confidently following a path to grow in the character of Christ.

Anyone who has ever studied a foreign language knows that continued practice is absolutely necessary lest all the time and effort to learn the language is lost. Proficiency follows regular, disciplined use of the language. The same is true of Christian discipleship. Unless followers are regularly learning from Jesus and applying those learnings in the exercise of their daily living and speech, any understanding of what a follower of Jesus looks like becomes blurred and, eventually, drops from sight. The primary goal of this spiritual formation process is to partner with you in language practice; to nudge each church member to recall, speak, and exercise what it means to be a disciple of Jesus. As Thomas G. Long so eloquently states it, "When we talk about our faith, we are not merely expressing our beliefs; we are coming more fully and clearly to believe. In short, we are always talking ourselves into being Christian."[3]

Small Group Session Format

Each of the eight one-hour small group sessions in this resource is divided into four sections, each building upon a single core thought. The aim is that, by working through these multiple channels of learning, you will be immersed into the core thought in such a manner that not only will you be equipped with head knowledge of the material but you will experience God's own activity in shaping your thoughts, desires, and values. Of course, the goal of this spiritual formation process is *living* a spiritual life. Each session is to be read and the assignments completed in their entirety prior to the small group meeting. The written assignments follow each of the first three sections of each lesson; the fourth section simply a meditation for personal reflection apart from the small group. The four sections of each small group session are:

- **Reflection** (allow 15 minutes) – A cognitive (*To Know*) exercise that provides a teaching based upon the core Scripture and core thought. This teaching is intended to provide a contemporary and relevant examination of the core thought challenging our values and lifestyle.

- **Life Story** (allow 15 minutes) – An affective (*To Feel*) exercise, these life stories have been prepared for this resource by pilgrims on their own faith journey and demonstrate the practice of the core thought in their journey. The intention of these life stories is that learners will appreciate the value of the particular faith practice in their own spiritual formation journey.

- **Equipping** (allow 20 minutes) – An exercise that directly asks for a behavioral (*To Do*) response to the lesson, this exercise explores deeply the core thought from the Scriptures. The aim in this exercise is not only to learn what the Bible teaches concerning the core thought but to faithfully respond to the teaching in one's conduct in life and practice of the Christian faith. Additionally, the practice of seeking God's counsel in Scripture models the basic Christian conviction that the Christian journey is informed by a regular study of God's Word.

---

[3] Thomas G. Long, *Testimony: Talking Ourselves into Being Christian* (San Francisco: Jossey-Bass, 2004), p. 7.

- **Closing Prayer** (allow 3 minutes) – Suggested prayer provided at the end of each session. Prayer may be read by the group or one person on behalf of the group.

- **Meditation** (allow 20-30 minutes of personal quiet time alone) - Presented to provide structure for time alone experiencing silence, solitude, and reflection. Intended for private devotional reading, each meditation continues reflection upon the core thought of the small group session. Read the meditation slowly. Note what insights, feelings, and nudges of the Holy Spirit you may experience. Simply sit quietly for 20-30 minutes reflecting on these experiences. Conclude by quietly thanking God for them and make a note of them in the margins of your book.

Time allotments for each portion of the small group sessions are provided as general guidance. The group, along with the group facilitator, will exercise discretion should meaningful conversation in one portion demand more time. Naturally, should one portion receive greater attention, time with another portion should be minimized to honor a one-hour time period for each group session. Each small group session closes with suggested activities for further growth: Spiritual Fitness Training. They are specifically designed to be a resource during the eighth and last session for the development of a Personal Growth Plan for the spiritual journey of faith.

Personal Preparation

During your time with the small group the group facilitator will guide group members through the reflection questions that were completed individually prior to the meeting. In addition to sharing your written insights, listen carefully to the insights and answers of the other members of your group. Answers of others should never be judged as incorrect. The reflection questions have been purposely crafted to seek one's personal engagement of the material, not evaluate one's grasp of the lesson.

Be prepared to write in your training manual anything fresh and new that you hear. This will increase the value of this resource for your personal spiritual growth. Acknowledge quietly to yourself throughout your preparation for the small group and during the small group meeting that Christ is very present, working to transform your thoughts and grow your heart. Weave prayer constantly throughout the process, asking that you not only experience the certain presence of the risen Christ but that you will be transformed by the Holy Spirit into Christlikeness.

Group Preparation

Identify a consistent time and place to engage this material as a small group. For example, consider meeting for an hour on fourteen consecutive Thursday evenings or Monday mornings or Sunday afternoons in a group member's living room, at a convenient coffee shop or a small room at your church. If the church is selected, be certain to reserve a place for the duration of this program to avoid the disappointment of discovering another ministry using your space at the appointed time of your group. Ideally, the group will begin at a time of the year where the fourteen sessions may be completed in continuous weeks with little or no interruptions, such as Christmas holidays or summer vacation.

A Brief Word for Facilitators

The primary responsibility of the facilitator of a Faith Journey Small Group is the recognition that you are not to teach this material. Members of the group are asked to complete all reading and written assignments prior to the meeting. Your function is that of facilitating helpful discussion and engagement of the material among members of your group – sharing your own responses to the questions in the material as you encourage mutual sharing by others. This will necessarily include maintaining a balance of participation by all members of the group – drawing out participation by the quieter members and helping more talkative members understand that others' insights are also valued. Every group member need not provide an answer to every question in each of the three sections of group study. As facilitator, simply ensure a balance of participation by every group member in the course of the one-hour session. An additional responsibility of the facilitator is keeping the group's members focused on the material and beginning and ending on time.

Final Remarks

It is my hope that this spiritual formation process finds a welcomed place in your yearning to experience Christ more intimately. It is a pathway that gently calls each one of us back to what truly satisfies – learning from Jesus, reordering our lives by those teachings, and experiencing His power for today and all of our tomorrows. As we grow and mature in discipleship, others will notice. And when we share what it is that is making a difference in our lives, we participate with the Holy Spirit in raising-up other disciples of Jesus Christ and the kingdom of God expands.

Additionally, there is the promise that, through each person who follows this pathway, the spiritual passion of the Church will be advanced and her preaching will result in the multiplication of the hands and feet of our Lord.

George Barna has written that discipleship is not a program. It is not a ministry. It is a life-long commitment to a lifestyle.[4] I would add that it is an exciting adventure with the one who created us, recovered life for us, and daily renews us. I look forward to sharing the journey with you.

---

[4] George Barna, *Growing True Disciples: New Strategies for Producing Genuine Followers of Christ* (Colorado Springs, Colorado: WaterBrook Press, 2001), 19.

SESSION 1

Entering into Community

Core Thought

The journey of the spiritual life must be a balance between time alone with God and time engaged with others who seek to be faithful. The spiritual life is neither a solo voyage nor one only developed in community with others. This lesson develops the value of the community dimension of the spiritual journey. Just as Christ moved within a small group of twelve men, small groups provide for each of us a dynamic and exciting community – a community where people from different backgrounds and life experiences can support and encourage one another while holding each person accountable for their own spiritual growth.

Core Objectives

- **To Know** (Cognitive):   An ability to summarize the role and value of a faith community in one's personal spiritual formation.

- **To Feel** (Affective):   Will value the richness of spiritual formation within community.

- **To Do** (Behavior):   Sign and follow through with a community covenant.

Core Scripture: *"So then you are no longer strangers and aliens, but you are citizens with the saints and also members of the household of God, built upon the foundation of the apostles and prophets, with Christ Jesus himself as the cornerstone. In him the whole structure is joined together and grows into a holy temple in the Lord; in whom you also are built together spiritually into a dwelling place for God.* (Ephesians 2:19-22 NRSV)

Reflection

The wildly popular reality show, "The Apprentice," permits a weekly glimpse at people who are being groomed by corporate success Donald Trump for an opportunity to manage one of his companies. Individuals are challenged to look deep within themselves, draw upon their own unique skills and talents, and place them before the mentorship of Trump as they are shaped into a remarkable story of success themselves. Some have said of the experience that here is an opportunity to become all that one is meant to be. All that is required is coaching and opportunity. "Apprenticeship" is all about becoming something more through the direct influence of another. God invites each of us to a holy apprenticeship – to experience spiritual formation through a faith community. The spiritual life is not a private process.

James C. Wilhoit states that, "Christian spiritual formation refers to the intentional communal process of growing in our relationship with God and becoming conformed to Christ through the power of the Holy Spirit."[5] There is much in that definition. It is dense and rich. One important observation is Wilhoit's use of the word, "communal." The Bible intends for spiritual formation to occur within community – with other people. Spiritual formation is not accomplished by private study or as a student in a classroom listening to the teaching of another. Both activities have value, of course. But they do little in shaping an individual into the character of Christ. That is simply because we have been intentioned by our Lord to grow spiritually in relationship with another. The Scriptures provide a sturdy foundation for this claim.

In Genesis 1-2, we read the account of Creation and God's purpose that we live in community: "It is not good that man should be alone" (Genesis 2:18a NRSV). For five days God is creating, and with each new thing God declares that it is good. Then on the sixth day God creates man, steps back, and God's appraisal changes. All was not as God intended. Absent for the man was a suitable creature that would provide "community." Creation is completed with the creation of woman who now "completes" man with the desired community. This community, writes the Apostle Paul in his letter to the church in Ephesus, is the very aim of God through history: the creation of an all-inclusive community of loving persons with God himself at the very center (Ephesians 2:19-22; 3:10), which is traced from the Garden of Eden all the way to the new heaven and the new earth (Revelation 21:1-5).

Life in community presents us with both a remarkable privilege and an awesome responsibility. Proverbs 27:17 tells us that "iron sharpens iron, and one person sharpens another." As other people's lives touch ours, they help to form our faith and make us who we are. As we touch others, we reflect God's love to them. The clear teaching of Proverbs is that God has ordained the making and growth of Godly men and women to be within community and to be the shared responsibility of all members of that community. Additionally, what becomes clear here in Proverbs is

---

[5] James C. Wilhoit, *Spiritual Formation as if the Church Mattered: Growing in Christ through Community* (Grand Rapids, MI: Baker Academic, 2008), 23.

that the mystery of the growth process is more "caught" than taught. The process of Christian spiritual formation goes infinitely beyond facts and information that can be acquired by individual study and reflection. The growth Paul speaks of here in Ephesians is imbibing a way of life that is embodied in a faith community. Joseph H. Hellerman states it most forcibility, "It is a simple but profound biblical reality that we both grow and thrive together or we do not grow much at all."[6]

The primary threat to community is what Eugene H. Peterson calls "The Brambles of Individualism."[7] It is the unique orientation of Western culture – especially contemporary American life – to go it alone; to embrace a strong sense of self-sufficiency and individualism. The result is people choosing to chart their own course through life, apart from a faith community, rather than integrating themselves into the body of Christ. The consequences are numerous: ill-conceived life decisions, lack of personal accountability, and bearing the pain of life alone. Additionally, pride is fostered in individualized programs of spiritual formation – the focus becoming one of outdistancing others.

Ephesians speaks to this individualism, by describing the Church, "which is his body, the fullness of him who fills all in all" (Ephesians 1:22-23). Not only has this letter from the hand of Paul been written to a community of believers in Ephesus and not to an individual, but Paul indicates that it is the Church that is the full expression of Christ. The image of the Church indicates that we are tied to one another and that each member is involved with all other members as together we go about doing Christ's work on earth. Any attempt to pursue the work of Christ separate from the body simply isn't supported by Scripture. We grow, mature, and serve within a community of other believers.

Relationships with other believers have extraordinary power in our lives because Jesus is present in them. Jesus knew the importance of people in conveying God's grace and presence. "Where two or three are gathered in my name," he said, "I am there among them" (Matthew 18:20). Within our churches, small groups, families, and friendships, we learn from one another. We find encouragement. We challenge one another to follow God more faithfully. Other Christians enable us to walk as we should when we might otherwise have strayed or wandered. God uses relationships to form us, and relationships form us so that God can use us.

Anne Lamott tells the story of her son's first year of life and the struggles she endured as a single mother and a recovering alcoholic. She writes about a particular day when she had reached the depths of exhaustion and depression and frustration with her newborn son; she had decided, somewhat facetiously, that it was totally crazy to believe in Christ. Then, she writes that something truly amazing happened. A man from the church where she worshipped showed up at the front door, smiling

---

[6] Joseph H. Hellerman, *When the Church Was a Family: Recapturing Jesus' Vision for Authentic Christian Community* (Nashville, TN: B&H Academic, 2009), 1.

[7] Eugene H. Peterson, *Practice Resurrection: A Conversation On Growing Up in Christ* (Grand Rapids, MI: William B. Eerdmans Publishing Company, 2010), 112.

and waving at Sam. A man in his fifties, he said that he wanted to do something for her and the baby. He asked her to imagine that a fairy had appeared on her doorstep and was prepared to do anything around the house, anything at all. After some coaxing, Anne finally answered that she would ask the fairy to clean the bathroom. The man from her church ended up spending an hour scrubbing the bathtub and toilet and sink with Ajax and hot water. Anne recalls that she sat on her couch while he worked, watching TV, nursing her son, Sam, to sleep, and feeling very guilty. But, she says, that kind of love made her feel sure of Christ again. I believe that what happened was that in the "community" that the church member brought to Anne's home, she once again experienced the certainty of Christ presence and love.

Reflection Guide

1. What are the biblical foundations for corporate spiritual formation?

2. Summarize the role and value of a faith community in personal spiritual formation.

3. According to Eugene H. Peterson, what is the primary threat to community in our culture?

4. From the reading, identify the negative consequences of a solo attempt at spiritual formation.

5. What can you do to move from an individualistic approach to spiritual formation to one that embraces community?

Life Story

Louis Sutton, Co-Executive Director, with his wife, Susan Sutton, WEC International
Prepared for this resource and used by permission of the author

10 pm is a strange and sleepy hour for a men's spiritual formation group, but for us as young college students in the 70s it was the time and place of our transformation. We were informed by our college studies, but we were transformed by that 10 pm group.

The group was born spontaneously from four guys who were new believers in Christ and who had strong desires to grow in their faith. We just figured that if we wanted to grow in Christ then why not use every tool God had provided for personal growth. And one of those "tools" is our brothers and sisters in Christ. Hebrews says "let us spur one another on to love and good deeds". So we made an informal commitment to "spurring" each other in the faith at 10 pm every night on the beat-up couches of the empty second floor lounge of the campus YMCA building.

The agenda was simple: share our hearts, challenge and encourage each other, pray for each other, and look at Scripture together. Some meetings were short. Some evenings we lingered together late into the night. Our commitment to other college groups came and went, but we never let go of that one. We remained committed to that group throughout all the years of college. Why? I think because God was using that group to change us. Thirty years later I don't remember much of the information from my college classes, but I continue to be impacted by the personal growth and lasting truths that were set in my soul those nights.

One of my most profound realizations of the nature of Christ happened in that little beat-up lounge. One of the members had just learned a new scriptural truth and shared it with the rest of us that night. He shared this truth very simply, but it impacted us all. In addition, one of the most challenging moments in my "sanctification" happened in that same room when one of the guys walked through the door with a new student he had invited to the study. New to everyone else, but not to me. In walked my arch-enemy from junior high school whom I had not seen since those conflicted days. The old "enemy" had also become a follower of Jesus and was attending our university. We now began a different kind of "engagement" in each other's lives!

The commitment to each other forged in the heights of the YMCA building has lasted. Seven years after graduation, we had a reunion and renewed that commitment, this time through a signed covenant. The document is now twenty-fic years old. The commitment still stands, and the paper remains in front of me. The first part reads:

Knowing that we have been made sons of God through the love and sacrifice of our Lord Jesus Christ;
Knowing that we are thus brothers in Christ;
Having experienced for a time the blessing of close daily fellowship with one another during our years at UNC-Chapel Hill;

23

Remembering especially our times of prayer together on the second floor of the "Y" building;

Realizing that God has significantly used our common friendship in each of our lives;

…we pledge ourselves…we covenant together …

We signed this covenant to continue to spur each other on even as our lives took us miles apart. In fact our paths did take us far apart as three of us became missionaries in Chad, Spain, and the Philippines. But the difference it made in our lives remains. Our simple commitment to be there for each other and to be a part of each other's growth in Christ was used by God for genuine transformation. Had I not been a part of that 10 pm group I might have had a few more hours of sleep or a few more hours of study, but I would have missed the transforming power of the spiritual formation group. God changed us, and He did so through a small group.

Take a moment and briefly write down anything you would like to discuss with your small group about this Life Story. What insights did you discover? What feelings did you experience? How did this Life Story increase your desire for living a deeper and more vibrant spiritual life?

Equipping: Proverbs 27:17

The metallurgical metaphor of iron sharpening iron illustrates the profound value of one person participating in the development of the godly character of another. The spiritual life is not something that is gotten for the wishing or assumed by the efforts of an individual. The spiritual life takes discipline and the "tough love" of direction and accountability of another.

Read Proverbs 27:17. *Write your answers below each question.*

" You use steel to sharpen steel — + 1 friend sharpens another"

1. Share with the group an experience where your own insights were "sharpened" and further developed by others.

2. Describe a time when poor personal decisions were lovingly called into question by another and a challenge was given to change your behavior. An example may be when a medical doctor or friend held you accountable to a better diet and exercise.

3. A common activity is two or more people studying together for an exam or exercising together to achieve some benchmark of physical wellbeing. What is the apparent value of these "communities" working together?

4. Psychologists tell us that we know ourselves as we know, and are known by, others. This is because the self refracted through another self becomes richer and more clearly understood. Have you experienced this to be true in your life? Describe this experience.

5. How has the reflection on this verse from Proverbs shaped your understanding of the value of spiritual formation within community?

6. What attitude will you change, action you will take, or prayer you will pray this week as you seek to share and experience God within the community of your church?

A Faith-Community Covenant

*With the intention of opening my life to spiritual formation and growth
I commit myself to the following:*

- Complete all assignments on a weekly basis prior to my Faith Journey group meeting in order to participate meaningfully.
- Attend each week unless there is an emergency that prevents my participation.
- Participate actively in the weekly discussion, sharing my reflections from the completed assignments.

- Contribute to a climate of honestly, trust, openness to the Holy Spirit, and mutual support and value of the other group members' comments and reflections.
- Maintain confidentiality of comments shared.

The above reflect the minimum standards for a productive and accountable process for spiritual formation. The group may add other elements to the covenant

Signed_____

Date_____

Closing Prayer

Prayer may be read by group or one person on behalf of the group.

We bind ourselves together, Lord, in the confident hope that through mutual accountability and the power of the Holy Spirit we may sharpen one another until we come to show the character of Christ in our lives. Amen.

Meditation

To be read devotionally apart from small group.

"Run in such a way that you may win"
(1 Corinthians 9:24 New Revised Standard Version).

The Apostle Paul frequently uses imagery from the early Olympic Games to illustrate the point of the Christian life. Here Paul compares the life of a Christian to running a race. And the point of both is the same: to win. Anyone running a race knows that to win demands a singular focus on the finish line. Stopping to check your pulse, to grab some refreshment, or look around at how others are doing simply distracts. Winning demands focus, and for the Christian that focus is the person of Jesus.

The difficulty for some Christians is that they have misunderstood where they should be in the Olympic Stadium. They have placed themselves in the grandstand or, rather, in the seats of the local church. They show up at the competition but not to compete. They show-up to watch, to be entertained. Some may even turn out to jog a couple of laps but little more. The Christian faith is reduced to a spectator's event that requires little effort. The sad result is a lack of personal transformation.

Paul is aware that competition is hard work. Perhaps that is why he uses the Olympic Games to make his point. Self-denial and grueling preparation are the order of the day for the athlete. For the person who is aiming for Jesus and his character, that means intentional practices as worship, prayer, Bible study and service. Such faith practices equip us to run the race with vigor and stamina. Winning a race requires purpose and discipline – and diligent training. But for those who run the race, the finish line is the embrace of Christ.

To Learn More:

Hellerman, Joseph H. *When the Church Was a Family: Recapturing Jesus' Vision for Authentic Christian Community*. Nashville, Tennessee: B&H Academic, 2009.

Smith, James Bryan. *The Good and Beautiful Community: Following the Spirit, Extending Grace, Demonstrating Love*. Downer Grove, Illinois: IVP Books, 2010.

Wilhoit, James C. *Spiritual Formation as if the Church Mattered: Growing in Christ through Community*. Grand Rapids, Michigan: Baker Academic, 2008.

SESSION 2

Understanding Discipleship

Core Thought

There are times when all of us simply go through the motions – just doing what needs to be done without any emotional engagement. This is also true for our spiritual lives. There is a dramatic difference between membership in a church and a vital and real relationship with Jesus Christ that grows and matures regularly.

Core Objectives

- **To Know** (Cognitive):   Write a personal definition of discipleship.

- **To Feel** (Affective):   Express your own sense of spiritual barrenness, your own hunger for a deeper faith.

- **To Do** (Behavior):   Identify personal habits, practices or attitudes that need to change as you seek to grow as a disciple of Jesus.

Core Scripture: "*For people will be lovers of themselves, lovers of money, boasters, arrogant, abusive, disobedient to their parents, ungrateful, unholy, inhuman, implacable, slanderers, profligates, brutes, haters of good, treacherous, reckless, swollen with conceit, lovers of pleasure rather than lovers of God, holding to the outward form of godliness but denying its power. Avoid them!* (2 Timothy 3:2-5 NRSV)."

Reflection

There is a prevailing assumption that authentic discipleship is hard and only for a few. Consequently, the church is populated with persons of faith who attend weekly services but whose lives give little evidence of being deeply affected or aroused by the hope of the gospel. Such a minimal experience of the faith denies the promise of Christ that he intends to give us life and that we shall have it abundantly. Such people may come to church but rarely do they come in an expectant mood. They betray their lack of expectancy by comments such as, "I only came to hear a good message." Theirs is a faith that may go through the outward appearance of practice but absent is any important change in their personal lives. This is mild religion and bears no resemblance to the church in the Book of Acts – the early church. If we want to see the kingdom of God and become animated by its power, we must open ourselves to radical renewal. The beginning place is an understanding of what discipleship is for the believer. The first exercise of this lesson is an exploration of some of the best wisdom on the question of discipleship – A Convergence of Wisdom about Discipleship.

A Convergence of Wisdom about Discipleship

In His Image

Discipleship means living a fully human life in this world in union with Jesus Christ and His people, growing in conformity to His image, and helping others to know and become like Jesus.

Michael J. Wilkins
In His Image: Reflecting Christ In Everyday Life (Colorado Springs, Colorado: NavPress, 1997), p. 55.

Transforming Discipleship

Discipleship means knowing him, loving him, believing in him, being committed to him.

Greg Ogden
Transforming Discipleship: Making Disciples a Few at a Time (Downers Grove, Illinois: InterVarsity Press, 2003), p. 76.

The Great Omission

A disciple is a learner, a student, an apprentice – a practitioner, even if only a beginner. In that context, disciples of Jesus are people who do not just profess certain views as their own but apply their growing understanding of life in the Kingdom of Heaven to every aspect of their life on earth.

Dallas Willard
The Great Omission (San Francisco: HarperSanFrancisco, 2006), p. xi.

The Disciple Making Church

Being a disciple means that you are one who trusts in and follows Jesus Christ, growing in his likeness and committing your heart, mind, soul and strength to obey and serve him.

Glenn McDonald
The Disciple Making Church (Grand Haven, Michigan: FaithWalk Publishers, 2007), p. xiii.

Traveling Together

…, a beginning point in describing a Christian disciple would be to say that this person is someone who desires to learn more about Jesus, so he or she can follow Jesus more fully.

Jeffery D. Jones
Traveling Together: A Guide for
Disciple-Forming Congregations
(Herndon, Virginia: The Alban
Institute, 2006), p. 41.

Discipleship Matters

Discipleship is the voluntary submission to the Lordship of Christ that results in the decision to learn from Christ, follow His example and participate in the expansion of God's Kingdom.

W. Douglas Hood, Jr.
Discipleship Matters, Vol. 2
Lenape Valley Presbyterian Church
New Britain, PA

From Members to Disciples

The expectations of discipleship are clarified and simplified: to be in a living relationship with Jesus Christ, to meet him in worship and personal practices of the faith, and to be in a community of living witnesses to his life-giving presence in our world.

Michael W. Foss
From Members to Disciples: Leadership
Lessons from the Book of Acts
(Nashville: Abingdon Press, 2007), p. 5.

Dissident Discipleship

"Jesus, what do you want me to do?" is the question that marks the first step of discipleship.

David Augsburger
Dissident Discipleship: A Spirituality of
Self-Surrender, Love of God, and Love
of Neighbor (Grand Rapids, Michigan:
Brazos Press, 2006), p. 31.

Growing True Disciples

Discipleship is not a program. It is not a ministry. It is a life-long commitment to a lifestyle.

George Barna
Growing True Disciples: New Strategies
for Producing Genuine Followers of
Christ (Colorado Springs, Colorado:
WaterBrook Press, 2001), p. 19

Disciple-Making Teachers

Fundamentally, the biblical word for "disciple" means learner or student. Of course, few people aspire to be lifelong students. Many become students for a short while, but generally as a means to an end. They usually have some larger goal in mind. But Jesus called us to be permanently in the classroom. The word "disciple" does not imply a static state. It implies someone who is growing, improving, reaching, stretching.

Josh Hunt with Dr. Larry Mays
Disciple-Making Teachers: How to
Equip Adults for Growth and Action
(Loveland, Colorado: Group, 1998), p. 13.

Renovation of the Heart

Rather, becoming a disciple is a matter of giving up your life as you have understood it to that point. Jesus made this starkly clear in Luke 14 and elsewhere. And without that "giving up," you cannot be his disciple, because you will still think you are in charge and just in need of a little help from Jesus for your project of a successful life.

Dallas Willard
Renovation of the Heart: Putting on the Character of Christ (Colorado Springs, Colorado: NavPress, 2002), p. 243.

Jesus of Nazareth

Again and again we are told that the crowd presses round him and follows him, and that Jesus can scarcely restrain them. They listen to him eagerly, amazed at the "authority" of his teaching; they seek his healing power for the sick; they praise the miracles he performs. Such is the general picture evoked by the Gospels, which serves as a frame for the innumerable individual scenes from the story of Jesus. These people, however, do not constitute his disciples. To follow somebody from place to place does not mean discipleship.

Gunther Bornkamm
Jesus of Nazareth (Minneapolis: Fortress Press, 1995), p. 144

The Shape of Faith to Come

For this study, disciple means "to be a learner and a follower of Jesus Christ." It implies obedience. It implies a lifestyle that demonstrates spiritual formation in terms of character and service. It means "to be like Christ." The word discipleship refers to a deliberate process of moving Christians forward spiritually.

Brad J. Waggoner
The Shape of Faith to Come: Spiritual Formation and the Future of Discipleship (Nashville, Tennessee: B & H Publishing Group, 2008), p. 14

Conversion in the New Testament

Discipleship begins, therefore, with the act of turning from rebellion against God (self-denial) and accepting instead God's will and way (cross bearing).

Richard V. Peace
Conversion in the New Testament: Paul and the Twelve (Grand Rapids, Michigan: Eerdmans, 1999), p. 256.

Reflection Study Guide

1. Which observation do you like best? Why? *Ogden (P. 29)*

2. What reoccurring themes do you notice? *learning*

3. What would you identify as the minimum requirements of discipleship?
   accepting God's way

4. With insights from this exercise write your own definition of discipleship.

5. What places of spiritual barrenness or hungers has this exercise brought forth within you?

Life Story

Susan Scott Sutton, Co-Executive Director, with her husband, Louis Sutton,
WEC International
Prepared for this resource and used
by permission of the author

A commercial in the 1960s featured a slogan that became a fixture of American pop culture. The commercial opens with a woman surrounded by chaos in her home. We can see her tension mounting until she utters the famous words, "Calgon, take me away!" The next scene shows her relaxing in a bath surrounded by quiet. The idea is that peace and restoration is only a bath product away.

The slogan came to mind more than a few times during our thirteen years as missionaries in Chad. Our home was "grand central station" with people coming and going at all hours. There were days when I felt closed in, not only by the physical walls surrounding our yard, but also by the busy-ness of our life. I often longed for a place where I could retreat in order to restore perspective.

There were two doors to our house. The front door was the center of activity. That was the door through which we met the outside world, where we welcomed visitors, interacted with merchants and beggars, and offered glasses filled with strong, sweet tea to drink with friends. The front door signaled by its openness that we were available to interact with anyone who came by.

The second door, directly opposite through the kitchen, led to a small backyard where we threw out dishwater and hung laundry to dry. Rarely did anyone walk around the house to the back door to find us.

One day in a desperate desire for relief from the demands of life at the front door, I exited the house through the back door, sat down on a rough wooden stool, leaned against the house and closed my eyes. When I opened them again and looked straight ahead, I saw only a cement wall, but when I looked up, I saw the sky.

There were birds flying overhead. I followed their unhurried movements on the warm currents of air and wished that I could sprout wings and fly with them, away from the demands waiting on the other side of the house. I opened the Bible I had grabbed on my way out of the door and read the following words: *But those who hope in the LORD will renew their strength. They will soar on wings like eagles; they will run and not grow weary, they will walk and not be faint (Isaiah 40:31).*

After a few moments of letting these words sink into my heart, my tangled thoughts unraveled, and I talked with God. I told Him what I was feeling, from the frustration of being little more than a pocketbook for constant requests for money to the weariness of handling a stream of visitors. And, to top it off, there was guilt. I was a missionary. Missionaries are loving and patient, and I was, most decidedly at that moment, not.

As I talked with God about how I felt, being real with Him and holding nothing back, the frustrations relaxed their clenching grip. Repentance pushed away the bad attitudes. Grace nudged away the guilt. A Father held his weary daughter. For that moment, I flew with the birds in the wide, open spaces, borne up by unseen currents of His spiritual air, and was soon able to return to the other door with renewed strength.

What changed me in those moments alone in the backyard? Taking a break from life's challenges? No doubt this helped. Stepping out of chaos into calm is a tried and true method for maintaining sanity, and I highly recommend it. But the truth is that real change came from a Person and not a place. What happened through the back door was a conversation and a re-connection. I spoke to God through prayer about what was on my mind and in my heart, holding nothing back – my part of the conversation. He spoke to me through His Word – also holding nothing back in His words that both encouraged and challenged me – His part of the conversation. Re-connecting with God in the middle of my hectic day restored my perspective and renewed my strength.

I realized in that afternoon that I don't need a physical place for peace and restoration, because I know a Person who is with me always. I just need to keep the door of my heart open to Him. Even while I am busy at the 'front door' of my public life that interacts with others in the home, in the office, at school, at the store or post office, I can at the same time step into His presence through the 'back door' of my heart. At any time and in any place, I can carry on a conversation with God and, in that moment with Him, be changed.

Take a moment and briefly write down anything you would like to discuss with your small group about this Life Story. What insights did you discover? What feelings did you experience? How did this Life Story increase your desire for living a deeper and more vibrant spiritual life?

Equipping: 2 Timothy 3:2-5

Paul is here concerned with those who have the appearance of godliness but whose inner attitudes of belief, love, and devotion to Jesus are lacking. If the inner qualities of a disciple of Christ are lacking, the outer appearance is meaningless. Paul warns us not to be deceived by such people – people who only appear to be Christians. More, the reader may discover that Paul's words speak to their own spiritual condition.

Read 2 Timothy 3:2-5. *Write your answers below each question.*

1. Paul's list of vices adds up to a "me-first" syndrome. What other vices do we see in our culture that demonstrates a "me-first" syndrome?

2. "Instant gratification" is a descriptor that is often used for the times we live in. How is this in conflict with Paul's desire that we be "lovers of God?"

3. Many pleasures are readily accessible, but love of God often requires effort. Briefly identify some of the effort that is required to nurture a love for God.

4. Paul's list of vices includes both obviously serious sin and others that our culture is often tempted to excuse as mere character flaws. Identify those vices from his list which are easily dismissed today as minor flaws and how they may be a hindrance to authentic discipleship.　　P 2S

5. In verse 5, Paul speaks of those who have the outward appearance of godliness – which can also be interpreted as "religion" or "faith" – yet deny its power. What Paul is saying here is that persons who have an authentic relationship with Jesus also experience Jesus' power that changes lives. Simply, going through the motions of faithfulness without evidence of a changed live is proof that an individual is a deceiver rather than a genuine disciple. They haven't opened

themselves to the power of God to transform them; they "deny its power." What habits, practices or attitudes might we have that "deny God's power" in our own lives?

Closing Prayer

Prayer may be read by the group or one person on behalf of the group.

O God, we come to you with our distractions, our differences, our disappointments and our secret hurts. We even come with our childish hostilities. We come as we are and ask you to transform each of us by your power that we may grow, day by day, into the image of Christ. Grant to us the understanding to know you, the diligence to seek you, the wisdom to find you, and the faithfulness to embrace you, through Jesus Christ our Lord. Amen.

Meditation

To be read devotionally apart from small group.

"Just say the word from where you are, and my servant will be healed. I know because I am under the authority of my superior officers, and I have authority over my soldiers. When Jesus heard this, he was amazed" (Luke 7:7-9 New Living Translation)

This passage startles us – a man of position and power comes to Jesus and asks him to give an order so his servant will be healed. Notice what the man doesn't ask of Jesus. He doesn't ask Jesus to come quickly to the bedside of the sick servant. He doesn't ask Jesus to touch the servant that he may receive healing. No. He simply asks that Jesus "give the order." That is enough.

What startles us is that this man, a man of authority, places himself under the authority of Jesus. More, he really believed that healing would come simply by the authority of Jesus' spoken word. The man's faith is not in what he wanted Jesus to do. Rather, his faith was in Jesus himself, whatever happened. He had faith to place himself under the authority of Jesus. This is the beginning place of discipleship.

This faith amazed Jesus. Perhaps Jesus was amazed because faith is so often misplaced. Often faith is rooted in a particular outcome. Healing is asked for and the test of faith is whether there is healing. This places Jesus under our authority.

What if we begin to rethink faith? Rather than thinking of faith as Jesus responding to our request, we are invited in this passage to submit to the authority of Jesus, regardless of the outcome of our prayers. This is what it means to truly be under the authority of Jesus.

We can't always understand Jesus. Sincere prayers are not always answered the way we would like. But we can trust Jesus. That is real faith. Believing in spite of what Jesus does. It is the kind of faith that will amaze Jesus.

Spiritual Fitness Training

Try one or more of the following Spiritual Fitness Training exercises and note whether it fosters spiritual growth. They may also be used in the development of your Personal Growth Plan during Session Eight.

1. Think through whom you would like to grow with you in your spiritual life. Pray for God to bring a few names to mind. Contact these people following these eight Faith Journey Small Group Sessions and invite them to share with you in a regular small group that focuses on spiritual transformation. Ask the pastor to help you identify appropriate curriculum for the small group.

2. Take a closer look at your life right now. Are there habits, practices, or attitudes that need to change as you seek to grow as a disciple of Jesus? Confess them to God in prayer and ask God's help.

To Learn More

Macchia, Stephen A. *Becoming a Healthy Disciple: 10 Traits of a Vital Christian.* Grand Rapids, Michigan: Baker Books, 2004.

Putman, David. *Breaking the Discipleship Code: Becoming a Missional Follower of Jesus.* Nashville, Tennessee: B&H Publishing Group, 2008.

Wilkins, Michael J. *In His Image: Reflecting Christ in Everyday Life.* Colorado Springs, Colorado: NavPress, 1997.

FaithPractice: Worship Regularly

❧

Worsh[...] [...] [...]od. It is a demonstration of [...] and again our lives on that which truly satisf[...] God in the person of Jesus Christ. Co[...] work[...] [...] [...]vice – to be instruments in the hands [...] [...]poses in the world. [...]

Handwritten note overlay:

Discipleship
④ Desire to learn more
5 - believe in J - Commit
② P.35
must put God 1st before self
③ resist all temptations
*   Godless*
⑤ Do not give our worries & fears
*   to God*

- **To Kn**[ow] [...] Summarize God's desire[...] for us in worship.

- **To Feel** (Affective): Will feel comp[...] experience worship more regularly.

- **To Do**: (Behavior): Reflectively read Revelation 4-5 and identify the places in worship you most readily connect with God. Attend worship regularly and take notice of parallels between worship in Revelation 4-5 and your experience."

Core Scripture: *"But the hour is coming, and is now here, when the true worshipers will worship the Father in spirit and truth, for the Father seeks such as these to worship him.* (John 4:23, 24 NRSV)

Reflection

We were created for worship. Everyone worships someone or something, perhaps multiple things at once. It is in our nature to assign ultimate value and worth to something beyond ourselves. The object of our worship may be the God disclosed in the Holy Scriptures of the Christian faith or any number of other gods of our fashioning. Even followers of Jesus Christ who gather regularly to worship him as Lord must confess that there are moments in life when our worship is directed to other things; we give ultimate value to money, a political party, a worthy cause or personal success. What is not always noticed is that the primary persons or things that receive our regular devotion ultimately shape our lives.

Here in John's Gospel, Jesus addresses a Samaritan woman and her question of location for worship; upon a mountain or in Jerusalem. Absent in the woman's concern about worship is any reference to who is being worshiped. Jesus rejects the traditional categories of worship location and redirects the woman's focus to the object of worship: "the Father." Far too often, the woman's condition is ours – we simply lose focus on the object of our worship, distracted by the many little things that matter very little. Such distractions for the modern Christian may be the style of worship, music preference, ascetic considerations of worship space, and quality of worship leadership. Though these considerations are not without importance, they are as distracting to God's desire for our worship as the woman's concern about location.

The difficulty with assigning ultimate value to matters or things other than "the Father" is that we lift up personal choice and preferences rather than Christ. Though it may appear subtle, the desire to shape worship to our liking actually diminishes authentic Christian worship. "The Father" is replaced by self in the preparation and delivery of worship. Rather than being transformed by the power of the Gospel, we continue participation in the culture that values self above all else. Jesus' lesson to the woman in John's Gospel – and to us – is that God desires in our worship for us to fall into the arms of God and say, "Here I am. There is no other place I'd rather be. Have your way with me."

Worship also restores an understanding of the source of all that is good, true, and beautiful. In a culture that values self-sufficiency and striving for more, Christian worship reminds us of who we are and that what we may become is not limited to our ability but is powerfully determined in the creative and redemptive power of God. Christian worship is an invitation to move beyond a work ethic to an experience ethic, to experience that God is in our midst and is the only real source of help in the troubles that most deeply impact our lives and the world. It is an invitation to a new orientation from presumption of one's own ability to a relationship with the Lord; a life orientation called for in Jesus' command, "Seek first the kingdom of God" (Matthew 6:33 NRSV).

The celebration of Christian worship, recognizing God's good desire for us, also speaks against the notion of scarcity that results in human striving for all things good, competition for one's own fair share, and finally evil towards others. Some years ago, I was provided with an unexpected (and what seemed an unorthodox) opportunity to explore this notion with my five-year-old son, Nathanael. He had again asked me to watch an episode of *The Simpsons* with him. Previous requests were resisted – certainly there were more fruitful ways to spend my time. It had been only a few months earlier that I acquiesced to his pleas that he be permitted to watch the show himself. The choice to spend time with my son that particular evening came down to playing Nintendo or watching this show with him. I watched *The Simpsons*.[8]

Homer, the father of this animated family, had found himself on the losing end of a bet that sent him packing to a tropical island as a Christian missionary. Asked by one of the indigenous people of the island why God needed people's worship, Homer's reply is, "Because he is an insecure God." Homer then resisted the people's effort to complete the building of a church begun by the previous missionary. Rather, Homer mobilized the people to build a Las Vegas-style casino – with gambling, entertainment, and inexpensive food. The result was self-indulgence, greed and, finally, the apparent self-destruction of the people. Realizing what he had brought to this once peaceful people, Homer began singlehandedly to build the church. Though unspoken, Homer and the island people then discovered that only in worship can we ever hope to experience wholeness and receive goodness.

Here, in this lesson from John's Gospel, Jesus seeks from the woman worship that preserves life from the destruction self-indulgent behavior would bring. God has the goal of goodness for all people and God's call to worship provides the hope that each of us will continue to experience blessings. My son's comment following this episode of *The Simpsons* will continue to be a treasure in my ministry: "Dad, worship really does matter!"

Reflection Guide

1 Summarize how you have experienced in your own life the experience of worship of someone or something other than God.

2. What have been distractions for you as you have shared in your church's corporate worship?

3. From the reflection you just read, summarize God's desire for us in worship.

---

[8] *The Simpsons*, "Missionary Impossible," #BABF11 / SI-1111 (originally aired February 20, 2000).

4. Summarize what Homer, the character from *The Simpsons*, apparently learned about the value of worship.

5. How might our worship protect us from self-indulgent behavior?

Life Story

Nancy Strickland, Elder, Lenape Valley Presbyterian Church, New Britain, PA
Prepared for this resource and used
by permission of the author

A Sunday morning service of worship is for me a gift of renewal, a reassurance of God's love – through the reading of Scripture, prayer, the sermon's lesson, and songs of praise, a surround of friends who give hugs and reaffirm my worth. The challenge begins immediately I leave the peace and focus of church for the world. I have to remember that the service of worship strengthens me for worship service: living my life as a disciple of Jesus Christ. Without worship service, a Sunday service of worship is empty. I'm trying to live God's guidance to Isaiah and Matthew: give food to the hungry, water to the thirsty, shelter to the wanderer, clothes to the naked; to end oppression, the pointing finger, the malicious talk. As my faith has deepened and the desire for discipleship grows, I'm trying actively to follow Jesus' direction to His disciples, "*to make disciples of all nations... teaching them to obey.*" In this discipline, I'm strengthened by Bill Hybels, a modern evangelist, who says that no one person is responsible for guiding the entire walk of another: helping through one step may be enough – others will come behind.

I started my worship service at church, reaching out – with mixed results – but I believe there were some very positive reactions – some small steps. For a short time this year, a young mother regularly brought her two young daughters to Sunday worship – then they stopped coming. I'd talked with her and felt her faith was fragile, but she was a believer, so I wrote her a couple of short notes, telling her how much I'd enjoyed meeting her and hoped she'd come back and worship with us. She did come back one Sunday, greeted me warmly and said my notes were the reason she was there! Right before Easter I sent her a well loved book by a woman missionary and Easter cards to the little girls. They all came for Easter Sunday! They've not been back since, but I'm still praying for them and writing my notes. I'm confident that God will guide them back to us or on to another church.

There's the bearded man in the red tow truck who hailed me by name in the convenience store packing lot one Saturday morning. He knew I didn't recognize him. Even after he introduced himself he had to recall meeting me at church several years ago – said I had been nice to him. Right: he attended irregularly with his wife and son, seemed uncomfortable in the sanctuary. But I insisted on greeting him whenever he showed up, striking up whatever conversation was possible in the short time before worship service. This family, like the young woman and her daughters, no longer come to our church, but I went home that Saturday and wrote a note to the man's wife; and I'm praying for them. I'm pretty sure they must be close to Him in some way because, after he gave me his business card and encouraged me to call him if ever I needed a tow, he said, "God bless you," before I could. I'm certain that if I ever need I tow I'll call him – and he will come and get me.

Away from church I read to preschoolers in a Head Start classroom, sharing a story, delighted by their exuberant participation. Recently I joined a new group determined to make a difference in our neighborhoods. Our first effort was collecting food for the local food larder – 2000 pounds in three hours from generous donors at area supermarkets! There is so much need in the world – I must keep my eyes open, my spirit focused on Him – and I must do the work!

Take a moment and briefly write down anything you would like to discuss with your small group about this Life Story. What insights did you discover? What feelings did you experience? How did this Life Story increase your desire for living a deeper and more vibrant spiritual life?

Equipping: Revelation 4-5

Revelation 4-5 provides a glimpse into the continuous activity of worship around the throne of God. It is here that the follower of Jesus is given a view of the future, our own eternal vocation in God's Kingdom.

Read Revelation 4-5. *Write your answers below each question.*

1. The first three chapters of Revelation are set on earth, specifically, on Patmos where John was in exile. In these three chapters John relates a vision where Christ came to him and instructed him to write to the seven churches. Now the drama

shifts, and John is transported to heaven. What John sees there he is also to "write in a book…and send to the seven churches" (1:11). In the fourth chapter John relates the continuous worship that surrounds the throne of God. In your own words, summarize what John experiences and writes of in the fourth chapter.

2. Summarize any parallels between John's vision of heavenly worship in chapter 4 and your own experience of worship. What are the differences?

3. What characteristics are ascribed to God in the fourth chapter?

4. John's vision shifts in the fifth chapter from the worship that surrounds the throne of God to the Lamb who is "worthy" of our worship. Summarize in your own words why the Lamb is considered "worthy" of our worship.

5. The vision of the fifth chapter clearly presents that it is the "slain" Lamb that merits the worship of the heavenly host. What does this suggest about the character of the lifestyle that is pleasing to God?

Closing Prayer
Prayer may be read by group or one person on behalf of the group.

Almighty God, strengthen us in our journey of faith, arouse in us a renewal of authentic worship and keep us from stumbling into lesser loyalties. Give us strength to stand firm in our hope in Jesus Christ, trusting in his grace and power for our lives. Amen.

Meditation

To be read devotionally apart from small group

"When they saw him, they worshiped him – but some of them still doubted!"
Matthew 28:17 (New Living Translation)

It is not unusual to have people share with me that they experience moments of doubt in their faith. Often in moments of suffering, despair, or hardship, they question, "Is it true?" What they want to know is if there really is a God and does God really care? The question is always asked in hopefulness; hope that their faith has not been for nothing. Unlike atheists, who refuse to accept the possibility of God, people who doubt genuinely want to believe – they are hungry for God.

It may help to realize that even some of the original disciples doubted. Men who had shared three years of their life with Christ, who had heard him say beforehand that he would be handed over to crucifixion, would die and, on the third day, be raised from the dead – some of them doubted. Doubt has always been a part of the Christian experience.

What is somewhat spectacular about this particular passage – a passage that acknowledges doubt among some of the disciples – is that it immediately precedes Jesus' sending the disciples out into the world. Jesus sends his disciples out, with their doubts and belief, to share the Christian faith. Apparently, unwavering faith isn't a requirement for evangelism.

A questioning faith doesn't seem to be a problem for worship either. It's clear in this passage that the doubts of some didn't stop them from worshiping Jesus.

It just may be that we are more troubled by our doubts than Jesus. Jesus is not dismayed by our doubts, but Jesus does want us to love him. Perhaps we have it all wrong. Rather than being troubled by doubts, we should be asking, "Do we love Jesus?" If we do, then, as the doubting disciples, let us worship him and be urgent in telling of his love to a hurting world. We may just discover our doubts swallowed up in the power of our worship.

Spiritual Fitness Training

Try one or more of the following Spiritual Fitness Training exercises and note whether it fosters spiritual growth. These exercises may also be used in the development of your Personal Growth Plan during Session Eight.

1. Public worship provides the opportunity for both experiencing the richness of God's character as well as our own celebration of God's love for us in Jesus Christ. In the next weeks of our time together, visit at least three traditions or styles of worship different from your own church. Keep a journal of how you experience God differently in the other church's worship. What feelings did you have about the services? What did you like? What didn't work for you? If you were on the worship committee of your church, what changes would you suggest?

2. Think of times when you experienced deep emotions in a particular service. What was happening in your life at the time? What, in particular, about the service was the most meaningful to you?

3. Resolve to be regular in worship the next six to ten weeks. Before each service, ask God to open you to experiencing God in new ways. Do not only pay attention to the leaders in worship but take notice of the other worshipers around you. How are they engaged? Is there a sense that they are in a holy place? Is there a note of joy and expectancy in their worship? From your observation of others in worship what do you sense about their own experience of worship? By the end of each Sunday, share with a spouse or friend what you experienced personally in worship and what you noticed about those with whom you worshiped.

To Learn More

Allen, Ronald & Gordon Borror. *Worship: Rediscovering the Missing Jewel.* Eugene, OR: Wipf and Stock Publishers, 1982.

Byars, Ronald P. *Christian Worship: Glorifying and Enjoying God.* Louisville, Kentucky: Geneva Press, 2000.

Dawn, Mara J. *Reaching Out Without Dumbing Down: A Theology of Worship for the Turn-of-the-Century Culture.* Grand Rapids, Michigan: William B. Eerdmans Publishing Company, 1995.

FaithPractice: Pray Daily

Core Thought

The spiritual life has to do with one's relationship with God. Prayer is the essential expression of this relationship. Prayer changes us and it changes God. Prayer changes us by directing us from self-reliance to trust in God and aligning our life with God's purposes. Prayer does not change God's nature but does change how God will direct God's power.

Core Objectives

- **To Know** (Cognitive):   Identify predominant cultural understanding of prayer and reflect upon a new biblical understanding.

- **To Feel** (Affective):   Will be encouraged to a more regular practice of prayer.

- **To Do** (Behavior):   Set apart a specific time and place each day where you ask God to participate in your life. What time of day will you pray and where will you pray without distraction?

Core Scripture: *"He came out and went, as was his custom, to the Mount of Olives; and the disciples followed him. When he reached the place, he said to them, 'Pray that you may not come into the time of trial.' Then he withdrew from them about a stone's throw, knelt down, and prayed, 'Father, if you are willing, remove this cup from me; yet, not my will but yours be done.' Then an angel from heaven appeared to him and gave him strength. In his anguish he prayed more earnestly, and his sweat became like great drops of blood falling down on the ground. When he got up from prayer, he came to the disciples and found them sleeping because of grief, and* *he said to them, 'Why are you sleeping? Get up and pray that you may not come into the time of trial'"* (Luke 22: 39-46 NRSV).

Reflection

The core Scripture is Luke's account of Jesus' prayer on the Mount of Olives. Though the first three Gospels report this story, only Luke develops the story to place the entire focus on Jesus. Matthew and Mark's focus is on the apathy of the disciples; Jesus came back to them three times and found them sleeping.

Luke has softened Matthew and Mark's rebuke of the disciples and explains their sleep as due to sorrow (Luke 22:45, 46). This change by Luke moves the attention of the reader to Jesus. Here, Jesus is not characterized as one who is eminently mortal, fallible, and vulnerable. New Testament scholar Luke Timothy Johnson observes that nowhere does this story reflect emotional tension or anguish of the soul. Rather, Jesus enters the struggle, much as an athlete engages in strenuous competition, his sweat not the physiological reaction to stress but a sign of his great effort. And his prayer demonstrates Jesus' awareness of God and the power of that awareness to strengthen. Fear and cowardice is shifted from Jesus to the disciples.

Jesus' struggle is not with fear but disobedience. It is a struggle of self-will that competes with God's will. Poignantly, this Scripture addresses the struggle of the popular culture with prayer. When prayer is approached today, it is often only after other resources to obtain what is wanted have failed. Prayer becomes the final expression of what is desired, reduced to a want list addressed to God. Here, the writer of this gospel invites the reader to another experience of prayer – to discover prayer as an opportunity of ecstasy that is experienced through a deep personal communion with God.

This alternative experience of prayer – one that is less about receiving and more about a heighten awareness of God – is brought forth poignantly by an article that appeared sometime ago in the Wall Street Journal. Here the Journal reported of a symposium held at Princeton on midlife career transitions. "There was a lot of solidarity around the question of what is next," commented one participant. Whereas prior generations often relinquished the tumult of youth for stability around the time they turned 40, midlife today increasingly involves starting over. The mantra of baby boomers – that work should be personally fulfilling – no longer satisfies and many feel propelled in middle age to risk following their deepest dreams. Striving for success is out of fashion; realizing significance is in. The kind of prayer Jesus engaged in on the Mount of Olives is prayer that pays attention to God and what God would have to do with us. This kind of prayer rarely changes our circumstances; it changes us.

Luke's treatment of the sleeping disciples also addresses the present culture's hunger for finding courage for life. I enjoyed a brief friendship with Bryant Kirkland, former pastor of the Fifth Avenue Presbyterian Church, New York City, before his death on Easter, 2000. He counseled me to listen to the city before attempting to preach to it. "Listen to its voice – to the needs, fears and concerns of those who live there." From his own listening, Kirkland found restless seekers of our post-traditional culture strolling through the spiritual marketplace in search of a God who makes life easier, rather than a God that offers courage to overcome life's difficulties. Every moment of life is pregnant with possibilities of both defeat and redemption. Enter the struggle alone and, like the disciples, one may become exhausted from grief and fall asleep. Yet, equipped with the discipline of prayer, we will not be overpowered. Joseph A. Fitzmyer, a Jesuit priest and scholar, suggests that the translation of verse 46 might be better served with: "What! Do you sleep?" Jesus expresses surprise that the disciples would so easily accept defeat rather than fortifying themselves through prayer.

Robert Wuthnow shares a helpful story of an individual who chose courage over despair. Mary Frances Housley was a young woman who lived in eastern Tennessee. One tragic day, she was witness to a plane crash in her community. Perhaps because she had once had a principal who talked about heroes, Mary Frances did not hesitate to enter a downed airplane to rescue whomever she could. She could have married, enjoying life as any other young wife except that she kept going back into that plane. Eleven times Mary Frances went back into the plane and that 11 times was just one time too many.

A crashed airplane is strictly for the stalwart men in asbestos suits and masks. It is not for the petite little Miss Pretty – not unless she is a Mary Frances Housley. Then she has such love in her heart that no high-octane explosion can ever blast it out.[9]

As we reflect on life in the twenty-first century, observes Wuthnow, we surely must hope that goodness and mercy, even of the extreme kind demonstrated by Mary Frances Housley, will be preserved. Yet, apart from the daily practice of prayer, few will experience the power and courage demonstrated by Housley. Luke invites the reader to stand steady and unshaken in the midst of life's turmoil. Jesus' prayer on the Mount of Olives demonstrates how.

This passage also addresses the faithfulness of God. Jesus did not have an easy course in his obedience nor will we. Many today are life-wearied. Tired, discouraged, and despairing, we find life does test our faith. In the midst of Jesus' own struggle on the Mount of Olives, Luke records an angel from heaven appearing to Jesus, strengthening him. In such times of physical and spiritual crisis, this passage calls us to follow Jesus more attentively – to seek God in prayer where we will be met by God's strength. And Luke wants us to hear, in a culture that demands more and more movement, and whose mindset is upon multi-tasking, that we are never so successful as when, like Jesus, we realize that God is present in all of our lives.

---

[9] Robert Wuthnow, *Christianity in the 21st Century: Reflections on the Challenges Ahead* (Oxford University Press, 1993), 57.

Success may be savored in one slice of life while despair claims another. God is present in both; God's faithfulness knows no boundary.

Reflection Guide

1. Jesus' prayer on the Mount of Olives occurs in Matthew, Mark, and Luke. What is the primary difference in Luke's version?

2. What tendency is observed in popular culture's use of prayer?

3. Joseph A. Fitzmyer has suggested a different way to translate Luke's version of this story. What is your opinion of his translation?

4. What questions do you have about the reading?

5. Has the reading changed how you will understand and practice prayer?

Life Story

Bruce Main, Executive Director, UrbanPromise Ministries
Prepared for this resource and used
by permission of the author

Friday morning chapel. The less-than-enthusiastic teenagers slouched into the room. It was 8:15 and everyone believed that even God wasn't awake till nine. Some placed their heads on their desks, not ready to deal with school yet. Others gossiped about weekend plans. It seemed unlikely there would be a reverential epiphany this morning. Teachers shushed the students. Chapel was just a chore.

"Listen to this sentence from the Bible,' began Mr. Bell tentatively. He doubted there would be any rustling of angel's wings this morning. He opened to an ear-marked page, slid his finger down the page and read in a deep, rich voice, *"Come to me, all of you who are weary and carry heavy burdens, and I will give you rest"*(Matthew 11:28 NRSV). He closed the Bible and leaned on the edge of the desk at the front of the room. He paused and intently looked at the sleepy, disinterested gathering.

"Do you have any burdens? Are you tired of carrying them?" It was like ice water tossed on them. The boys in the back defensively snickered, hoping to rally the others.

Mr. Bell: "Settle down, guys."

Awkward silence came over the room. Mr. Bell waited.

"My younger sister moved out of the house last week," began 14 year old Sheena in practically a whisper. One of the back boys muttered, "Good for her," provoking chuckles. But Sheena was not deterred. "She's living with my dad and I'm concerned for her safety. I don't get to see her." Sheena began to cry. Nobody in the room breathed.

Another hand shot up. "I'm worried about my mom," voiced Shamar, "She has two jobs and she still can't keep up…she's under a lot of pressure."

Joseph interrupted. "My mom's always locked in her room; I can't get her to come out. She's really stressed. I hate to see her like that."

For the next 30 minutes the students poured out their hearts to one another and their teachers – sharing their burdens and telling of the things that really wearied them. Those rough edged teens hugged one another, cried with one another, and prayed for each other. In those sacred moments they were safe. They had become the church for each other.

The apostle Paul wrote to the Church of Galatia that they should "bear one another's burdens, and in that way fulfill the law of Christ." The law of Christ? Why did Paul use such weighty language when describing the act of carrying one another's burdens? Perhaps because Paul realized that the health and vitality of the Christian community was somehow linked to this unique Christian practice of looking beyond ourselves and sharing the pain of our brothers and sisters.

Our kids demonstrate something powerful for us all. They show us that we may not be able to eliminate our burdens and our worries, but we can bear them together as we respond to Jesus' invitation to come to him in prayer – they can become a little lighter, a little easier to manage.

Take a moment and briefly write down anything you would like to discuss with your small group about this Life Story. What insights did you discover? What feelings did you experience? How did this Life Story increase your desire for living a deeper and more vibrant spiritual life?

Equipping: Matthew 6:5-8

Jesus provides instruction here about prayer with an emphasis on the contrast between genuine and hypocritical approaches. Jesus rails against ornamental prayers. Such prayers have more to do with drawing the favor of people than building a relationship with God. Authentic prayer is to be done simply and in the privacy of one's one room.

Read Matthew 6:5-8. *Write your answers below each question.*

1. What does Jesus say about the prayers of the hypocrites?

2. Summarize Jesus' instruction on prayer.

3. Jesus cautions, "do not heap up empty phrases as the Gentiles do (Matt. 6:7)." Thomas G. Long suggests that "the target is not lengthy prayers per se, but what could be called 'safecracker' prayers; that is, windy and fawning prayers that attempt to use flowery charm to pick the lock on the favor of the gods, to manip-

ulate the gods into action by uttering the right combination of words."[10] How does Long's comment alter, if at all, your understanding of the character of God?

4. Jesus tells us that the Father already knows what we need before we ask. What difference, if any, does this make on your prayer life?

5. Someone once said that this model of prayer is really asking God to participate in your life. How would you ask God to specifically participate in your life this week?

Closing Prayer
Prayer may be read by group or one person on behalf of the group.

Grant to us this week your certain presence in our moments of prayer. Help us enter each day in the joy of the Lord and retire in the evening certain of your protective embrace. Amen.

---

[10] Thomas G. Long, *Matthew* (Louisville, KY: Westminster John Knox Press, 1997), 68.

Meditation

To be read devotionally apart from small group

"We always thank God for all of you and pray for you constantly."
I Thessalonians 1:2 (New Living Translation)

I received a powerful and warm e-mail recently. A woman took a moment from her workday to tell me that on Saturday evenings she pauses to pray for me. She remembers a comment I made once that Saturday evening is the time I get off alone to walk through my neighborhood and reflect on the sermon I will deliver the next morning. "Just wanted to thank you for being my pastor and let you know that each Saturday I pray for you as you reflect on your sermon."

Perhaps you can appreciate the extreme joy I felt when I read those words. The bond between this woman and me grew a little stronger. Her note also reminded me that the Christian faith is not a solo voyage; we share together in the life of faith with other believers and with the Lord.

Paul knows this, of course. Here, Paul continues to build a bond with a new Christian community that he had started only months earlier. He begins reminiscing about the time he had been with them and the warm thoughts that well up in his heart burst forth in thanksgiving. Yet, as Paul's words continue, he moves beyond giving thanks and mentions that he prays for them constantly. The Thessalonians are new at the Christian faith and have much to learn. Paul hopes to encourage them and be a source of strength along their journey with Christ.

Prayer is the binding force of the worldwide fellowship of Christians. Constant prayer for one another has the capacity to brush away the tarnish of disagreements, misunderstandings, and little hurts that would diminish the quality of our relationship with one another. Curiously, the development of a regular network of prayer relationships promises to build a church that is invincible to the sin in each of us that would destroy it. Perhaps constant prayer for one another should be a priority for every Christian.

Spiritual Fitness Training

Try one or more of the following Spiritual Fitness Training exercises and note whether it fosters spiritual growth. They may also be used in the development of your Personal Growth Plan during Session Eight.

1. Purchase an inexpensive journal and record daily prayer thoughts. Follow the progression of your thoughts over a period of time. Do your prayers express adoration, confession, thanksgiving, requests for others as well as yourself?

2. Join a prayer group that meets regularly for prayer.

3. Attend a prayer retreat.

4. Read a book on prayer. Keep a journal or writing pad near for recording insights and questions.

To Learn More

Cedar, Paul. *A Life of Prayer: Cultivating the Inner Life of the Christian Leader.* Nashville, Tennessee: Word Publishing, 1998.

Foster, Richard J. *Prayer: Finding the Heart's True Home.* San Francisco: HarperSanFrancisco, 1992.

Yancey, Philip. *Prayer: Does It Make Any Difference?* Grand Rapids, Michigan: Zondervan, 2006.

SESSION 5

FaithPractice: Learn and Apply God's Word

Core Thought

Central to the thought and practice of the Christian faith is God's Word. We read God's Word, along with practice of other Christian disciplines, for spiritual transformation. God's Word transforms our world view, reorders our priorities, shapes our behavior and empowers the heart for abundant expressions and demonstrations of love and forgiveness. Reading God's Word replaces old destructive habits with life-giving habits. God's Word reshapes people, distorted by the world, to be the people of God we were created to be.

Core Objectives

- **To Know** (Cognitive):   Know why a regular and attentive reading of Scripture can be beneficial to our spiritual formation.

- **To Feel** (Affective):   Cherish the richness and benefit of the regular reading of God's Word.

- **To Do** (Behavior):   Begin to make connections between what is learned in Scripture and application of learning's in your personal life; to make "life application" in your reading of Scripture.

Core Scripture: *"The tempter came and said to him, 'If you are the Son of God, command these stones to become loaves of bread.' But he answered, 'It is written, 'One does not live by bread alone, but by every word that comes from the mouth of God.'"* (Matthew 4:3, 4 NRSV)

Reflection

Perhaps it's no surprise the number of persons today who think they know the Bible but, in fact, have absorbed mistaken notions popular today. For instance, parents are sometimes heard telling their children the story of Adam and Eve. As the story unfolds, an apple appears – and often it is a bright red apple. Truth is there was no apple in Eden. The story of Adam and Eve doesn't even mention "forbidden fruit." What the Bible does say is that Adam and Eve were not to eat the fruit of the tree in the middle of the garden, the tree of knowledge of good and evil.

There are other widely held beliefs about the Bible that are equally mistaken: Joseph's garment was not a "coat of many colors" but, rather, a long robe with sleeves" and we really have no idea how many wise men came to adore the Christ-child. Matthew's Gospel simply states that there were three kinds of gifts brought by them. It seems apparent in the larger church that knowledge of the Bible is shaped more by what is heard than what is read.

Many of the mistakes heard today don't really compromise our faith. They may be untrue, but it would be difficult to argue that they are harmful to the witness of the church. And it may be that, by politely pointing them out, curiosity will propel people to read the Bible and discover a whole new world of understanding.

While these mistakes may be harmless, they do point to a great danger, the potential for mistaken notions of who is the living God. Idolatry – the creation of some image of God that becomes the focus of our devotion and worship – is kept on a very occasional and loose leash. There is a robust sense that ours is a culture that is given more to forging gods that will serve personal and ambitious goals than honestly – and without qualification – engaging the God of the Bible.

We live today in a world of options and choices and gods who enchant us with promises. Walter Brueggemann, a prominent Old Testament scholar, suggests that what Israel sought during Moses' absence in the wilderness was not a representation of God through the golden calf but another god that would powerfully grant material desires.[11] The commandment against idolatry in the Book of Exodus explores whether our love for God is for who God is or for the things God is able to give us. The Middle Eastern world with all of its physical representations of gods has narrowed the church's understanding of this commandment. Idols can be fashioned by the mind and will more lavishly than by the hand. To seek after a god who is nothing more than the great giver is to have fallen before a graven image in worship; it is to practice idolatry. Lack of faith, or the disturbance of faith, becomes the dark symptom of this worship when what is sought is not received.

A personal experience may be helpful. At the beginning of my sophomore year of college, my parents bought me my first car – a canary yellow Pontiac Firebird Formula. They purchased the car on a Wednesday prior to the Saturday I would

---

[11] Walter Brueggemann, "Theology of the Old Testament" (Class lecture, Columbia Theological Seminary, 1986).

fly to London for the fall semester. For four months, all I had of that new car was a Polaroid. When my father picked me up at the airport he did so in my new car. Finally, after four months I would enjoy driving my Firebird. He suggested that rather than going straight home we stop by the beach. It was late in the evening and few people remained. My father and I parked the car and began walking together along the shore. It was then that I realized what I had missed more during those four months was not my car but being with my father. It is good sometimes to honestly examine the character of our love for God; do we love God or simply the things that God can give us?

This passage from Matthew's Gospel invites God's people to discover that our deepest desires are not met in anything but intimacy with God, the God disclosed to us in God's Word. Jesus is out in the wilderness. He has been there for a considerable period of time and is now hungry. The devil reminds Jesus of his power and his ability to grant the desires of his stomach. He responds to the temptation by calling upon God's word in Deuteronomy 8: "Man does not live by bread alone, but he lives by every word that proceeds out of the mouth of God." As Jesus speaks those words here in Matthew 4, he has in mind both the historical back-story of Deuteronomy 8 and the larger purposes of God. Jesus wants us to hear that God desires for us exceed our immediate appetites.

One way to hear Jesus' words here in the fourth chapter of Matthew is to listen to them juxtaposed with his words on prayer in the sixth chapter, "Give us this day our daily bread." Jesus wants us to pray for daily bread realizing that it is essential to life but that, alone, it isn't sufficient for the life God intends us to have. What we really need is a different kind of bread – the words of life from God. Each one of us has been created in a manner that we require spiritual food as well as physical food. God's word is bread that satisfies the human heart and soul and Jesus wants us to be aware of our need for this bread every day.

Reflection Guide

1. The reading provides several examples of mistaken beliefs in popular culture about the content of the Bible. Identify any other mistakes you have heard about what is found in the Bible.

   a. forbidden fruit – not apple
   b. Joseph's coat of many colors – long robe w/ sleeves
   c. # wise men? – brought 3 differ gifts

2. Idolatry is defined in the reading as some image of God we fashion that becomes the focus of our devotion and worship. Identify any idolatry that has been active in your own life.

3. Imagine that you are teaching a Bible study on the core Scripture passage, Matthew 4:3, 4. How would you make a "life application" of this passage to your students?

4. Identify a time when a particular passage of Scripture was helpful or nourishing to you in your life.

5. Share how this reading has provided you with fresh insights about the practice of regularly reading and applying God's word to your life.

Life Story

Jim Mignard, elder, Lenape Valley Presbyterian Church, New Britain, PA
Prepared for this resource and used
by permission of the author

Nobody's perfect. Not even the cast in the Bible. Adam was disobedient, and Noah drank too much. Isaac was weak-kneed, and Jacob a scoundrel. David committed adultery and plotted murder, and Solomon his son set a record for womanizing. Job went bankrupt. Jeremiah spent most of his life whining and complaining. Rahab was a hooker, and Peter a coward.

And God loved all of them.

He loves me, too, but at times I forget this. When I get grumpy (a part of my personality, I'm afraid), I'm uplifted when I turn to the Bible and *allow God* to remind me again that I'm in his hands, as is my family.

Despite a testy disposition, I have a desire to live in a way that pleases God—nothing is more important than that—and that catches his eye and shows him that I trust his promises. When finances are tight, for example, and worry begins to pull, I rest in Jesus' encouragement in Matthew 6:25-34. He mentions "worry" or "anxiety" six times as *unnecessary* emotions for God's children. He urges me to bank on what he's saying because he knows what our heavenly Father can do.

Have you ever thought of taking one—just one—of the promises in the Bible, memorizing it so you can recite it easily, then telling God, that as a follower of his Son, you want to please him by relying on that promise?

Consider forgiveness. Then turn to Mark 11:25 (or Matthew 6:14-15) for one of Jesus' promises on the link between divine and human forgiveness. The happiest person I have ever met was an Episcopal chaplain with the RAF during World War 2. I asked him about his cheerfulness, and he just said, "I'm on the ins with God and on the outs with nobody." That's Jesus' promise in living color!

At the age of 84, I think a bit more about heaven than on what career I should be preparing for. But regardless of age, immerse yourself in Jesus' promise in the Gospel of John, chapter 14. It's for everyone. Jesus speaks: "Don't be troubled. You trust God, now trust in me.... I am going to prepare a place for you" (New Living Translation).

When Jesus went through a severe testing (Matthew, chapter 4), he held up by reminding himself, three times, that his Father's promises were written down in black and white and he could trust them. And that grueling hour in the desert is itself described three times in the New Testament so that we won't miss the point: we also can find relief when life is tough *by doing what Jesus did.*

He passed the test, but how? He recalled Scripture: "*One does not live by bread alone, but by every word that comes from the mouth of God.*" (NRSV) Or as the New Living Translation puts it: "*The Scriptures say, 'People need more than bread for their life; they must feed on every word of God.'*"

I'm glad that I don't have to try to win God's approval for eternal life; I couldn't do it anyway. But if God in his mercy, love, and forgiveness has accepted the Rahabs, Noahs, and king Davids of the world, he can also bring me into his family. And now that I'm a family member, I want to follow, as best I can, the teachings and examples of his Son. I can do that by listening to him each day in the Bible.

Take a moment and briefly write down anything you would like to discuss with your small group about this Life Story. What insights did you discover? What

feelings did you experience? How did this Life Story increase your desire for living a deeper and more vibrant spiritual life?

Equipping: Psalm 119:105

Considered by many to be one of the most beautiful strophes in all of the Psalms, this verse aptly characterizes Israel's understanding of God's word – that God's instruction lays out the pathway for the faithful to walk. Rather than viewing God's word as an instrument for correcting the wrong doer, Scripture assists in the correct use of individual freedom, identifying dangers along the way of life and offering direction, encouragement, and strength for life's journey.

Read Psalm 119:105. *Write your answers below each question.*

1. Psalm 119 is the longest of the psalms, and there is hardly a verse that does not contain a reference to God's word and law. In this verse, the metaphor of "light" is used to indicate that God's word is a reliable guide to life. Read through Psalm 119 and list other metaphors used for God's word and law.

2. Which metaphor best describes your present experience of the Bible. Explain.

3. James Limburg writes that Psalm 119 is designed for people who understand life to be a journey through territory that is not their homeland. In other words, this is a psalm for persons who understand themselves as sojourners.[12] This segment assumes that our journey is through darkness (see Ps. 23:4). In such a situation,

---

[12] James Limburg, *Psalms: Westminster Bible Companion* (Louisville, KY: Westminster John Knox Press, 2000), 413.

the Lord's word is like a flashlight, suggests Limburg, helping one find the way. "Darkness" becomes a metaphor, including personal affliction (v. 107) as well as attacks from certain wicked persons (v. 110).[13] Describe a period of "darkness" in your life and how God's word provided guidance and comfort.

4. What does this verse suggest will be the result in our lives if we use God's word for direction in our daily steps?

    have an edge on our enemies
    we become wiser by doing what you tell us
    avoid detours from route you laid out

5. Rewrite this verse in your own words.

    God's light is a realiable guide to life (question #1)

Closing Prayer

Prayer may be read by group or by one person on behalf of the group.

Heavenly Father, through your Word you made all things in heaven and on earth. By your Word you have opened to us the path from death to life. Sustain us today, and all of our tomorrows, by the words of Holy Scripture that our love for you may increase even as we discover more deeply your love for us; through Jesus Christ our Lord. Amen.

---

[13] Limburg, *Psalms*, 417.

Meditation

To be read devotionally apart from small group

"I have hidden your word in my heart, that I might not sin against you."
Psalm 119:11 (New Living Translation)

It isn't unusual for me, as a pastor, to hear people say that they can be good Christians without reading the Bible. "After all," they argue, "my life doesn't allow such a luxury. Full-time career, spouse, parent, and keeping a home demand all that I have. There simply isn't anything left over to give to reading the Bible." Yet, they continue, they are good Christians, never cheating on taxes, loving to their families, and showing kindness to the stranger.

Certainly, these are the marks of a good person. And the world would be a better place with more of them. What seems to be overlooked, however, is that there are non-Christians who are also good people. What makes one Christian cannot be boiled down to being a good person. To be Christian literally means one who seeks to bear the image of Christ. This is far deeper and richer than simply being good.

To claim the title, Christian, means that we seek to have our lives directed, driven, and dominated by Jesus. That means who we are and who we will be is not for us, or the world, to determine. Christians submit their lives to be determined by Jesus – the Jesus revealed in the Bible. Reading the Bible, then, becomes an act of submission. We submit ourselves to be molded into the image of Christ by God's word. No other word can make us Christian.

This, of course, is sometimes threatening. If we are use to the words of the popular culture that we should get what we deserve, then the words of the Bible will appear strange, even subversive, when they speak of sacrifice. But then, William Willimon, popular author and teacher, has said that those who genuinely seek to be Christian will appear to the world a peculiar people.

Perhaps there is no sin greater than not becoming who we were created to be, a biblical people shaped into the image of Christ. But if we read the Bible, if we hide the Word of God away in our hearts, we will one day discover that we have become Christians!

Spiritual Fitness Training

Try one or more of the following Spiritual Fitness Training exercises and note whether it fosters spiritual growth. They may also be used in the development of your Personal Growth Plan during Session Eight.

1. Explore different ways of listening to Scripture.
   - Read short passages of the Bible out loud and slowly. Listen carefully to the words. Which words or thoughts resonate most meaningfully to you? Keep a journal of these words and thoughts. Reflect on them throughout the day.
   - Print a short Bible passage on a card and place it on your desk or work station. Read it throughout the day, reflecting on its application to your life.
   - Have the pastor suggest an appropriate commentary on a book of the Bible of your choice and read it, along with the corresponding book of the Bible. Exercise care that you don't try to read too much or read to rapidly. The goal is to read slowly and reflectively, asking God in prayer to make connection points between the Word of Scripture, the scholarship of the commentary, and your life.
   - Select a short Book of the Bible, or a portion of a longer book, and create an outline of the book, noting characters, places, action, lessons that are taught.
   - Listen to the Bible on CD while you work around the house or drive.

2. Join a Sunday school class or small group that specifically studies the Bible. Record in a journal any insights that you discover and any application to your life that are revealed.

3. Listen carefully to the sermons in worship for the next weeks of our time together. Make notes of the Bible passage that is preached on, helpful illustrations that are used, the lesson or lessons that are communicated, and any call to personal action that may be in the sermon. Following the worship, read the sermon passage alone. Are there other insights that you discover not addressed in the sermon? What other connection points to your own life do you find?

To Learn More

Fee, Gordon D. & Douglas Stuart. *How to Read the Bible for All It's Worth*. Grand Rapids, Michigan: Zondervan, 2003.

Foster, Richard J. *Life With God: Reading the Bible for Spiritual Transformation*. San Francisco: HarperOne, 2008.

Mulholland, Jr., M. Robert. *Shaped By The Word: The Power of Scripture in Spiritual Formation*. Nashville: Upper Room Boos, 2000.

SESSION 6

FaithPractice: Participate in a Ministry

Core Thought

Implanted deep within the nature of men and women is the hunger to serve others. Those who receive love discover a need to love. Those who receive ministry experience a compulsion to minister to others. Through loving others and participating in a ministry, we discover a depth and vitality of faith that cannot be experienced otherwise. Indeed, we discover that the promise of Ephesians is certain and true, that as each one of us engages in the work of ministry, we shall all experience a maturity of faith, even to "the measure of the full stature of Christ" (Ephesians 4:13).

Core Scripture: *"The gifts he gave were that some would be apostles, some prophets, some evangelist, some pastors and teachers, to equip the saints for the work of ministry, for building up the body of Christ, until all of us come to the unity of the faith and of the knowledge of the Son of God, to maturity, to the measure of the full stature of Christ"* (Ephesians 4:11-13 NRSV).

Core Objectives

- **To Know** (Cognitive):   Enhanced clarity concerning the nature and purpose of spiritual gifts for spiritual formation and growth.

- **To Feel** (Affective):   Challenged to identify a personal ministry within the church.

- **To Do** (Behavior):   Demonstrate personal faith through personal actions and participation in a ministry of the church.

Reflection

In an engaging and insightful book, *Creative Spirituality: The Way of the Heart*, Robert Wuthnow identifies some of the criticisms that have been voiced in recent years about spirituality in the broader culture. "One of the most reoccurring criticisms is that too many Americans shop around for spiritual cues, rather than settling into communities of faith where they can learn discipline or serve others. Spiritual seeking draws criticism because it seems to reflect a shallow consumerist mentality."[14] Against this consumerist mentality, Ephesians announces that an authentic relationship with God is rooted in a personal engagement in all that God is doing in the world. Quick routes to personal gratification may be an easier course to navigate, but it is a pilgrimage that is unknown in Scripture and one that fails to encounter the deep mysteries of faith.

If there is to be a recovery of a reawakened faith, the experience of expectancy and power of Christ in daily life, all who are Christians must be engaged in some kind of ministry. The old-fashioned idea that ministry is a professional matter must be abandoned. Elton Trueblood once remarked in a sermon that, "Religion is like medicine. There is a sense in which both are good for everybody, but they are dangerous in both instances, unless they are administered by those who have the professional stamp upon them."[15] The vitality of early Christianity was not primarily due to a few brilliant leaders; instead, it arose because the idea of non-ministering Christians was unanimously rejected. Engagement in ministry results in the sense that we belong to something great, that we are connected to something larger than ourselves.

Peter J. Gomes, minister emeritus at Harvard's Memorial Church, spoke of the prevailing sense of emptiness in our culture to the editors of *Harvard Business Review*. In that conversation, Gomes shared that he often crossed paths with successful people in business at just the point where they are asking questions such as, "What's it all worth? What am I getting out of this? What have I done? I'm successful by every standard this world can imagine, and yet I'm unhappy. Or I can't produce happiness in others. How do I reconcile my success with my sense of emptiness?" Gomes says that such individuals have put their ultimate confidence in penultimate enterprises. "Business has to be a means, not an end. If you treat success in business as life's ultimate goal, then it becomes a great, glowering, impressive, but ultimately empty and futile, tin god."[16]

---

[14] Robert Wuthnow, *Creative Spirituality: The Way of the Heart* (Berkeley, CA: University of California Press, 2001), 269.

[15] Elton Trueblood, *The Yoke of Christ and Other Sermons* (New York: Harper & Brothers, 1958), 139.

[16] Peter J. Gomes, "Is Success a Sin? A Conversation with the Reverend Peter J. Gomes," *Harvard Business Review*, September 2001.

The contemporary soul wrestles with the spiritual anxiety of claiming meaning despite the press of meaninglessness that is very pervasive in our lives. Ephesians invites such fragmented anxieties to be brought to Jesus where they are woven into a bold and confident purpose. Discovery of God's purpose for each of us and active engagement in that purpose gives birth to a truly aroused faith. Consider what Kenneth C. Haugk says about God's call to every person to participate in a ministry:

> The depth and vitality of faith shows in the actions of the faithful. When people experience God's overwhelming love, they are compelled to share it through their words and their deeds by using their spiritual gifts. When people's needs for spirituality, community, and care are met, they overflow with gratitude and love   for God and others. The abundance spills over in deeds of ministry. People need to minister. They long to share the thankfulness, joy, and understanding they have with those in need. Individuals are eager to be involved in ministries that use their gifts.[17]

When people are invited to participate in a project larger than their individual selves, what emerges is a far greater Christianity – a greater Christianity than one that restricts ministry to a few.

This brings us to another point. As good a definition of practical Christianity as you will find comes from the Book of James. It is this: Faith by itself, if it has no works, is dead. That comes from James' second chapter, and what it is saying is that, when God comes to judge us, the question is not going to be whether we were obedient to the law, or whether we made a profession of faith in Jesus Christ. The question is going to be ultimately whether there exists any evidence of faith, whether in our lives there is fruit of lives given over to a new orientation because of Jesus. The new orientation that God will be looking for is a life that has given itself away in ministry to others as Jesus lived his own life.

Ephesians urgently calls us to discover that the maturity of faith God desires for us is within our grasp. The pathway is made clear. You and I are gifted people – gifted for the work of ministry. In this world a common mantra that has emerged is that we are not to become overly committed, to stay on balance and keep our lives for ourselves. In this worldview, the writer to the Ephesians sticks out like a stray dog that has wandered into our living room during a party. "I am a prisoner of the Lord (Ephesians 4:1)." It takes a person who has spent considerable time listening to God to recognize that placing one's gifts at the disposal of the church is not only a divine commandment, it is ultimately how we are able to keep our lives from slipping into meaninglessness and despair.

---

[17] Kenneth C. Haugk, *Discovering God's Vision for Your Life: You and Your Spiritual Gifts*, Participant Manual (St. Louis: Tebunah Ministries, 1998), 130.

Reflection Guide

1. Restate, in your own words, the primary criticism that Robert Wuthnow identifies about spirituality in the broader culture.

2. To what extent is this criticism true of your own spiritual journey?

3. Summarize Ephesians' antidote to a superficial, consumerist spirituality.

4. Peter J. Gomes, speaking to the editors of *Harvard Business Review*, said that business has to be a means, not an end, if happiness is to be realized. Summarize your understanding of what he is saying.

5. Express in your own words the Book of James' understanding of practical Christianity.

6. Share how this reading has provided you with fresh insights about the practice of participating in a ministry.

7. The faith practices of worship regularly, pray daily, and learn and apply God's Word have little value, says the Book of James, if "it doesn't result in faithful activity" (James 2:17 Common English Bible). Why is "faithful activity" or participation in a ministry important for one's spiritual growth?

Life Story

James Hodsden, Head of Staff, Ardmore Presbyterian Church
Ardmore, PA
Prepared for this resource and used
by permission of the author

The Central American sun beat down upon the workers outside of a small Christian school in Belize. I was sweating as I slathered wet cement on top of a cinderblock. I was among a group of Americans on a mission trip who had flown down to help the school with whatever needed doing. What needed doing that morning was building some columns and extending the roof of the classrooms. My qualifications for the job were primarily that I was there. Masonry is not a skill or talent that I would ever list on a resume. Nonetheless, here I was, carefully tapping another cinderblock into place. Suddenly, I was passed by a flock of children running toward a field. It was time for recess. An impromptu soccer game began, but one young boy stayed behind. He watched me intently as I did my assigned job. At home, his first language was Spanish, but he offered a critique in perfect English,

"This must be your first time that you've ever done this." As I reviewed my work, I hadn't realized that my inexperience showed. We both laughed.

In terms of simple finances, the mission trip would be a failure. The money it cost to send unqualified people to do work in a faraway place could have been used elsewhere. However, the laugh that we shared made all the difference. We would not be bringing Jesus to Belize. Instead, ministry is about joining God already at work. When we go to serve, we show the world that Christ is not divided by culture or geography. Our faith deepens when our relationship with Christ develops into relationships with the people we serve. Ministry becomes an avenue for spiritual growth.

All of the Americans who came on this mission trip brought different talents and different motivations. In the context of our work, we were drawn closer to God and to each other. God's purpose became clearer as we worked together. We recognized our ministry partners here and abroad as brothers and sisters in Christ. We saw a glimpse of God's faithfulness, and we were able to recognize it again when we saw it in our daily lives.

An amazing thing is that we don't have to join God in a place overseas. Jesus wants to be with us in our homes, schools, and workplaces. We work out our faith in the context of our lives. It is no wonder that James writes, "Faith without works is dead" (James 2:17). The lives we lead are expressions of the faith we have. God simply created us to do ministry.

Take a moment and briefly write down anything you would like to discuss with your small group about this Life Story. What insights did you discover? What feelings did you experience? How did this Life Story increase your desire for living a deeper and more vibrant spiritual life?

Equipping: James 2:14-26

The Book of James is widely regarded as a kind of how-to manual for the Christian life. Here in this passage, James explores the relationship between faith and works, developing his theology by means of explanation, humor, and illustration.

Read James 2:14-26. *Write your answers below each question.*

1. What is James' understanding of the relationship between *faith* and *works*?

2. Some suggest that verse 2:19 is a rather humorous illustration by James: "You believe that God is one; you do well. Even the demons believe – and shudder." James's point is that only believing the right things makes little difference in our life – even the demons believe the right things! Faith is more than right belief. Genuine faith that changes lives is enacted in works, which are its proper expression. How has this insight changed your understanding of God's call upon you to participate in a ministry?

3. James provides us with two examples of "faith in action:" Abraham and his willingness to offer his son Isaac as a sacrifice to God and Rahab, a prostitute, whose faith in God moved her to protect Israelite spies. Share your own example of someone who, through their actions, demonstrated their faith in God.

4. James closes this portion of his letter with another illustration: "For just as the body without the spirit is dead, so faith without works is also dead" (James 2:26 NRSV). In this context, "spirit" means "breath." James intends for the reader to hear that, just as "breathing" is a sign that the body is alive, so are "works" a sign of the presence of faith. Write in your own words what James is trying to say.

5. Martin Luther, the leader of the Protestant Movement, once remarked, "I almost feel like throwing Jimmy (the Book of James) into the stove."[18] Luther's concern was that readers of James would mistake James' teaching on "works" as the means by which we are made right with God. What the careful reader of James discovers is that, while we are made right with God only through trusting in Jesus Christ

---

[18] Frances Taylor Gench, *Hebrews and James* (Louisville, KY: Westminster John Knox Press, 1996), 104.

as Savior (faith), our works are the demonstration of that faith. How would you explain this to a new believer?

Closing Prayer

Prayer may be read by the group or by one person on behalf of the group.

Heavenly Father, you meant that our faith should be alive and vital, full of wonder and power. Give us today a vision of how you intend to use us for your purposes that we may experience a full maturity of faith, even to the full stature of Christ. Amen.

Meditation

To be read devotionally apart from small group.

"...for it is God who is at work in you, enabling you both to will and to work for his good pleasure." Philippians 2:13 (New Revised Standard Version)

Someone once cautioned that Christians must avoid the anxiety of doing God's work for him. In other words, we are all gifted and called to participate in God's work in the world, but only in partnership with God. There is vast difference in doing work for someone and participating with them in a work. God may send us out into the world but we are reminded in the Great Commission, "I am with you always." Our work on behalf of God's kingdom is always done with God.

The prophet Isaiah understood this. Speaking through Isaiah, God tells us, "You are my witnesses." It's the job of witnesses to point away from themselves to another, in this case, to what God is doing. And understanding this, we can release ourselves from the anxiety that we are responsible for the salvation of the world. That would make us a savior, but not Jesus.

What the apostle Paul wants us to hear, however, is that God's activity in the world is largely through people like you and me – people who are committed to Jesus. As we are called and sent to participate with God in ministry, we are asked to notice that it is God who enables all that we do. Our ministry is a shared one, shared with one another and God.

The question then becomes, "Are you paying attention to God?" The Psalms instruct us to "Be still, and know that I am God" (Psalms 46:10a). It is only when we pay attention to God that we discover that we are invited to a partnership with him in all the work that remains to be done in the world. A follower of Jesus who is not involved in some ministry is simply a contradiction.

Spiritual Fitness Training

Try one or more of the following Spiritual Fitness Training exercises and note whether it fosters spiritual growth. They may also be used in the development of your Personal Growth Plan during Session Eight.

1. Explore opportunities in your congregation for volunteering in a ministry. You may want to speak to the pastor or a Volunteer Coordinator if your congregation has one. Among the opportunities that are available, pray that God will direct you to one that seems right for your interests and abilities. Begin by making small commitments until you have discerned if that particular ministry seems right for you.

2. Sign on to be part of a team to set up or tear down for an event in the church such as special dinners, special worship services, and similar activities. Usually a congregation has the greatest difficulty identifying people for such tasks. Make a mental note of what it was like to be of service to the church in this manner. What do your feelings/thoughts tell you about being used by God in this way?

3. Keep a journal of ministry activities that you participate in. Who did you meet? What ministry did you provide? How did you feel upon the completion of the ministry? Exhilarated? Sense of personal worth? Exhausted? Not the right ministry for me?

To Learn More

Mallory, Sue. *The Equipping Church: Serving Together to Transform Lives*. Grand Rapids, Michigan: Zondervan, 2001.

Ogden, Greg. *Unfinished Business: Returning the Ministry to the People of God*. Grand Rapids, Michigan: Zondervan, 2003.

Ott, E. Stanley. *Transform Your Church With Ministry Teams*. Grand Rapids, Michigan: William B. Eerdmans Publishing Company, 2004.

FaithPractice: Give Financially to the Ministry of the Church

Core Thought

Giving financially to the work of the church has little to do with meeting the needs of the church and a great deal to do with one's own progress in the spiritual life. Wealth can be a significant impediment to discipleship blocking our way to God. Responsible financial giving to the ministry of the church is a demonstration that we trust, finally, not in our personal resources to hold together our future but the power and gracious activity of God.

Core Objectives

- **To Know** (Cognitive): To state the value of responsible financial stewardship for personal spiritual growth.

- **To Feel** (Affective): An increased desire for responsible financial giving to the ministry of the church.

- **To Do** (Behavior): Look thoughtfully and prayerfully at present giving to the church and demonstrate a commitment to grow in sacrificial giving.

Core Scripture: *"But the father said to his slaves, 'Quickly, bring out a robe – the best one – and put it on him; put a ring on his finger and sandals on his feet. And get the fatted calf and kill it, and let us eat and celebrate; for this son of mine was dead and is alive again; he was lost and is found!' And they began to celebrate"* (Luke 15:22 NRSV).

Reflection

The story of the prodigal may be read from many different angles, none more poignant than the extravagant, squandering grace of the father. Squandering grace is a fairly good place to begin thinking about financial giving to the ministry of the church. That is because we are called as disciples of Jesus Christ to respond with extravagant gratitude to the extraordinary gift of life. As God's people struggle to grasp the magnitude of God's grace, they are changed from a people who "store up for themselves" into a "squandering people," who generously release financial resources in active participation with God in God's redemptive work in the world.

This parable of the lost son primarily addresses personal relationships: our relationship with God, one another, and with our financial resources. The present culture of affluence challenges disciples to an honest assessment of those relationships. A look at where we invest our time and money may move us toward observations that are unsettling. Were the parable of the lost son set in the present day, we might find him investing time and money in the pursuit of distinctive cars, luxury vacations, and cashmere socks. As one someone once observed, "I have not made a life for myself; I have purchased a life for myself."[19]

Another, yet equally compelling, dynamic that may be found in this parable is the quality of those relationships. While the lost son invested time in the pursuit of an abundant life materially, the son that remained home did so bitterly. This bitter alienation of the other son represents a loss of another kind – a broken relationship with family. It is a loss that is harder to recover than the loss of material wealth. One can reasonably assert that surrendering your Visa card is more honest, and less hurtful, than the pretense of continuing in a relationship that one deeply resents. The tragedy of the older son is his failure to cultivate a satisfying relationship with the father. The difficulty was that he remained focused on that portion of the inheritance squandered by his younger brother. Though he remained on the old homestead, his heart drifted far way.

This parable challenges a culture of consumerism with God's claim on our checkbooks and lives. It is a parable that invites reflection and consideration of what really matters to us. Our checkbooks will answer whether we are organized around a particular lifestyle or if our lives are focused on celebration and thanksgiving. The true poignancy of the parable of the lost son is that both sons were far from the father and, consequently, both hungry - the one son who squandered his inheritance on extravagant living and the other who "stored up treasure" for himself. The father goes out to both, one on the road returning home and to the other in the field for he won't come into the home. For both, the father provides comfort. God's claim on our checkbook isn't for the balance noted on the ledger. It is the

---

[19] David Remnick, ed., *The New Gilded Age – The New Yorker Looks at the Culture of Affluence* (New York: Random House Trade, 2000).

Father again on the road and in the field seeking to reclaim hearts held in bondage to the checkbook balance.

Congregations and their members who approach financial stewardship from a biblical perspective do not view the money they give to their church merely as a way to cover the necessary expenses of providing ministry. Rather, such members understand that, as followers of Jesus Christ, financial giving to the ministry of the church is an act of discipleship, a tangible means of growing spiritually. By supporting the church and its mission and ministry with a percentage of their incomes, they demonstrate the high value they hold in participating in the activity of God in their community and the world.

Reflection Guide

1. Share how you have seen the misuse of wealth damaging relationships within families and with God. Avoid disclosing the names of individuals.

2. In your own life, which character in this story do you most identify with: the father, the son who stayed home, or the prodigal son? Explain.

3. Briefly identify the difference between a lifestyle driven by culture and one driven by discipleship.

4. To what extent has your own spiritual journey been hindered or advanced by your personal giving?

5. What is there about money that it has the power to injure relationships?

6. Does the seductive power of money frighten you? Explain.

7. How has this reading spoken to you this week?

Life Story

Al DeVries
Prepared for this resource and used
by permission of the author

I have always been a Christian. My father was Assistant Supervisor of the junior department and a deacon in a large Presbyterian church in a suburb of Newark, New Jersey. My mother was a member of a Southern Baptist Church in Newark, New Jersey. I don't ever remember not going to Sunday school. When I got old enough, I started going to church after Sunday school with my dad. He would give me ten or fifteen cents to put in the plate as it came past. When I was about 10 years old, I accepted Christ as my savior.

After I came back from the Army, I sort of drifted away from church. None of my friends went to church, and we always seemed to have something else to do on Sunday. If there were nothing to do, I would go to church with my Dad. I was working and would throw a buck in the collection plate; made me feel like a big man as I was supporting the church.

In 1952, the insurance company I worked for was opening an office in Jacksonville, Florida. I talked it over with Mary and we decided I should ask for a transfer. I did and was accepted.

A number of the people I worked with in Jacksonville belonged to a Southern Baptist church in Jacksonville. This church televised their Sunday morning service live, and I started turning it on to find out if I would see anyone I knew. Then, on Monday morning, I would go to work and say, "Hey, saw you on TV yesterday," and I always got the same reply, "Why don't you come and join us, and you, too, can be on TV." So I did.

Up to that time I had never heard the word "tithe," or, if I had, I'd let it slip over my head. Once a year, the pastors of this church would preach "tithing" for three or four weeks, and then everyone in the church would turn in their slip telling how much their tithe would be that year. I thought "there is no way I can give 10% of my money, I'm just getting by as it is." The pastors, Dr. Lindsay and Dr. Vines, kept telling all of us to, "try it for one month and see what will happen." I would not take the chance.

Although I worked full-time for the insurance company, Mary and I opened a florist business at home specializing in orchids. We belonged to an organization that would sponsor orchid shows in malls all over the state. These were three-day affairs, set up on Friday morning, sell Friday, Saturday, and Sunday, tear down on Sunday night, and go home. I had an old Dodge van I would load up on Wednesday night, leave early Thursday morning, and drive to where the show was to be held. I would find a trailer park and rent a space to park for the time I was going to be there.

There was a show in Miami, and I was staying at a county-run park about 10 miles from the mall. It was Sunday morning, and I was on my way to the mall when the oil light came on. Instant panic! I pulled over and crawled under the van to find out the oil pressure switch had blown out and was leaking oil all over the engine. Here I was 400 miles from home with a broken down van on a Sunday morning. What to do??

I know you are not supposed to bargain with God, but I got back in the van and prayed, " Lord, if you will help me out of this, I will start, this week, tithing all the profits from these sales." The campground where I was staying had given me a paper with its rules and some business advertisements on it. I had put it on the console in the van, and, as I looked down at it, there was an ad for an auto parts store that was open on Sunday, and it was on my way to the mall. This just doesn't happen. I drove there, and they had the part. I replaced the bad switch and drove home that night.

The next morning, I told Mary about the deal I had made with God and she said, "How do you know how much is 10%? You have to figure in the cost of heat, supplies, etc." My answer to that was simple, "We know how much I left with and we know how much I came home with. So we take 10% of the difference." From that day, on we were tithers, but only on what we made from floral sales. Funny thing,... floral sales just kept getting bigger and bigger, and with it our 10%.

After about six months of this, we were talking about it and Mary said, "What do you suppose would happen if we started tithing on ALL of our income?" We started that week and have never stopped, and anytime we NEEDED money it has always been there for us. Note that I say, "needed," I don't think if you said, "God, I need a Rolls Royce or a Lincoln Town Car," you would get it, but when the rent is due I'm sure it would somehow get there.

A friend and I were talking and the subject of tithing came up and he told me this story. He was down to his last $10.00 one Sunday morning and had been laid off from his job. He had a wife and two kids. The question in his mind that day was, "Do I give God his tithe or should I keep that one dollar?" Only God would know if he kept it. He made his decision and gave God his dollar. That afternoon his union boss called and offered him the foreman position on a big project that would last all winter. You figure.

Take a moment and briefly write down anything you would like to discuss with your small group about this Life Story. What insights did you discover? What feelings did you experience? How did this Life Story increase your desire for living a deeper and more vibrant spiritual life?

Equipping: Luke 12:13-21

Responding to an anonymous question put to him, Jesus offers a parable that addresses attitudes and actions concerning possessions. Most immediately, Jesus looks to draw from the crowd insight about what our practices concerning material wealth proclaim about our understanding of God and God's promises. Jesus' hope is that disciples will be released from the fear of scarcity, thus the need to gather and hoard wealth, and enabled to reorder their lives toward active participation in God's work in the world.

Read Luke 12:13-21. *Write your answers below each question.*

1. The prevailing assumption in our culture is that life does in fact consist of one's possessions. In your own words, how does Jesus address that assumption?

2. The question placed to Jesus is really about fairness; the fair distribution of an inheritance. Jesus' response is one of refusal to act as a "holy" referee but, rather, he uses the question to reflect deeply about the accumulation of wealth. Identify

how you have observed a desire to accumulate wealth negatively impacting individuals, families, and communities.

3. Tom Wright, reflecting on this passage, states that the world seems to thrive on people setting higher and higher goals for themselves, and each other, so that they can worry all day and all year about whether they will reach them. If they do, they will set new ones. If they don't, they will feel they've failed. Wright asks, "Was this really how we were supposed to live?"[20]

4. Briefly describe the man's attitude in Jesus' parable as he talks to himself in verses 17-19. Have you ever seen this attitude in yourself? Explain how you feel now.

5. Anxiety about wealth reflects a lack of trust in God as well as a lack of generosity toward others. Have you ever given so generously that you felt "pinched" or "hampered" in your personal finances? Describe how you felt after making that sacrificial gift.

---

[20] Tom Wright, *Luke for Everyone* (Louisville, KY: Westminster John Knox Press, 2004), 151.

Closing Prayer

Prayer may be read by the group or one person on behalf of the group.

Almighty God, so draw our hearts to you and so direct our minds that our ultimate trust may be found in your love and not in the treasure we accumulate. Show us how to manage our money that we show concern for the poor and advance your work in our community and the world; though our Lord and Savior Jesus Christ.

Meditation

To be read devotionally apart from small group.

"For where your treasure is, there your heart will be also." Matthew 6:21 NRSV

For many of us, this passage is so familiar that we no longer hear it at all. We understand it, and there is nothing more to be said. It is a straightforward, simple comment from the lips of Jesus. Yet, this passage presents a difficulty for the church. It is one of the most misunderstood Scriptures in the New Testament. Perhaps a closer reading of it is in order.

What we think we hear goes something like this: "Wherever your heart is, there will your treasure be." That's what we hear because that's a truth that "goes without saying." We all know, from personal experience, that where our heart is, there will be our treasure.

Photography is a passionate hobby of mine. I may never be the professional that my father was, but I enjoy everything about the art of photography: the different kinds of cameras, the particular uses of various lenses, the study of light and composition and on and on. Without question, it is where my heart is…and, consequently, a good deal of my treasure.

But look again at the words of Jesus. He didn't say, "Wherever your heart is, there will your treasure be." He knows that's true. It's obvious. No, he reversed the image. Jesus speaks first about treasure and then matters of the heart. What Jesus wants us to hear is that, wherever we place our treasure, our heart will follow. That is also true, isn't it? Place your treasure in the stock market and you will discover that you follow the market very carefully.

What Jesus is offering us is an opportunity to grow closer to Him. If we desire a closer walk with Jesus try placing a "treasure" of your resources in the offering plate. This, of course, is more than the small change you will never miss. The heart rarely follows small pocket change. And when you do give, you will discover that your heart has grown closer to Jesus. It's a matter of investing first where you want your heart to be…because it will certainly follow!

Spiritual Fitness Training

Try one or more of the following Spiritual Fitness Training exercises and note whether it fosters spiritual growth. They may also be used in the development of your Personal Growth Plan during Session Eight.

1. Daily, for the next weeks of this journey together, ask God in prayer to speak to you about your management of money. Seek God's direction in your giving to the ministry of the church. Particularly consider giving a percentage of your income to the church rather than arbitrarily settling upon some amount. Develop a plan to increase this percentage until you have reached the biblical standard of ten percent.

2. Maintain a journal over the next weeks of this journey together where you record the amount of your weekly giving to the church, including amounts to special giving opportunities. Include reflections of your feelings about each gift – were your feelings those of duty or of joy? Did participation in some special gifts touch you deeply? How might you continue to give in ways that increase joy?

3. Participate in a church sponsored financial management seminar on responsible Christian management of your money. As your debt decreases from responsible management, consider increasing your giving to the ministry of the church.

4. Read the book, *The Stewardship of Life: Making the Most of All That You Have and All That You Are* by Kirk Nowery (published by Spire Resources, Inc.) or a similar book on stewardship, and maintain a journal of lessons learned, reflections that you have, and questions. At the end of your reading, share with the congregation, written for the newsletter or orally in a worship service, how you have grown from the reading and changed your attitude about giving to the church.

To Learn More

Gill, Ben. *Stewardship: The Biblical Basis for Living*. Arlington, Texas: The Summit Publishing Group, 1996.

Witherington III, Ben. *Jesus and Money: A Guide for Times of Financial Crisis*. Grand Rapids, Michigan: Brazos Press, 2010.

SESSION 8

Charting the Journey

Core Thought

Dallas Willard, noted speaker and author in discipleship, writes that it is unlikely that followers of Jesus will experience a satisfying relationship with him without the vision, intention, and means to do so. The casual and haphazard practice of faith of so many usually results in a faith that lacks vitality and joy. What is required is some intentional commitment and reorganization in our own lives.

Core Objectives

- **To Know** (Cognitive):   Define present strengths and growth areas in the five faith practices.

- **To Feel** (Affective):   Confidently know the next steps in your faith journey toward putting on the character of Christ.

- **To Do** (Behavior):   Construct a Personal Growth Plan from the Spiritual Fitness Training suggestions for identified faith practice requiring growth.

Core Scripture: *"Let us throw off everything that hinders and the sin that so easily entangles, and let us run with perseverance the race marked out for us"* (Hebrews 12:1 NRSV).

Reflection

Following Jesus is an intentional decision followed by intentional activity. A plan for spiritual growth must be placed alongside appropriate support and the accountability of a small faith community; otherwise our spirituality grows only in a confused and disorderly way. Absent a plan for growth, support, and accountability, the beauty of our lives becomes disfigured by the forces of our culture; the quality of our relationships with one another and God is diminished. Structure, support, and accountability give us the freedom and place to grow as we were meant to be. Dallas Willard states it best, "The ultimate freedom we have as human beings is the power to select what we will allow or require our minds to dwell upon."[21] A Personal Growth Plan can be a great help in realizing the growth God desires for each of us.

Personal plans for spiritual growth may be developed in many different ways. Ideally, a plan will be developed by the individual embarking on a journey of spiritual growth with consideration given to one's particular needs or growth areas at the present moment. During this small group session, you will identify at least one of the faith practices we have studied in which you recognize your need for personal growth: a place where you seek God's gift of freedom from particular barriers to living as a fully committed follower of Jesus Christ. You will then develop a Personal Growth Plan with weekly check-in for the next six weeks from the Spiritual Fitness Training found at the end of the appropriate session previously studied. A commitment to pursue such a plan will help you experience God's transforming work in that faith practice. The result will be a spiritual journey far more satisfying than one left to the malnourishment of selecting particular activities at the church that seem interesting.

During the time that you pursue your personal growth plan, you will journey with a specific roadmap that provides structure, support, and accountability. This road map significantly increases the possibility that the journey will be a fruitful one. The roadmap may be thought of as "Three Points of Engagement for The Journey." Each of these points of engagement will provide the structure or framework for your spiritual formation: 1) Time Apart - actively pursuing the selected Spiritual Fitness Training exercises and intentionally practicing a regular time of silence and solitude, 2) Time in Community – for the purposes of continued study of discipleship in the Scriptures and the giving and receiving of support, encouragement, and accountability, and 3) Time Sharing – following the personal growth plan, sharing with one other person your personal experience of growth. Consider it this way. The particular Spiritual Fitness Training exercises you select for your personal growth plan will be the "content" of your faith journey, the three points of engagement will be the "structure or shape" your journey will take.

The anticipated outcome of this adult formation program is that you will discover that following Jesus and living as his disciple is more than attendance at church functions. Transformed lives is the result of Jesus active within hearts and minds of people who are captive to the story of Jesus' life, death, and resurrec-

---

[21] Dallas Willard, *Renovation of the Heart: Putting On the Character of Christ* (Colorado Springs, CO: NavPress, 2002), 95.

tion and who intentionally pursue a pathway for growing in obedience to all Jesus taught. My hope is that you will find in this adult spiritual formation process the spiritual resources to meet the challenges and pressures that confront each of us daily and you will move from exhaustion and defeated lives to victorious living. Henry Ward Beecher once commented, "Religion means work. Religion means work in a dirty world. Religion means peril; blows given, but blows taken as well. Religion means transformation. The world is to be cleaned by somebody and you are not called of God if you are ashamed to scour and scrub."[22] Perhaps a succinct statement of an anticipated outcome, as suggested by Beecher's words, is an ever increasing number of persons equipped and committed to the missional work of God in the world.

Take a moment and briefly write down anything you would like to discus with your small group about this reflection. What insights did you discover? What challenged you? What questions do you have?

Personal Assessment of Your FaithPractice

The following assessment tool will help you create a Personal Growth Plan that is best suited for your particular needs and growth areas. By answering the following questions, you will identify both your present strengths and your opportunities for growth. After you have answered all the questions, you will recognize the one or two faith practices of discipleship that require an intentional plan for growth. They will be the ones that received the largest number of "no" answers. Once the one or two faith practices that require growth are identified, simply return to the end of those small group sessions and select two or three Spiritual Fitness Training exercises that make the most sense for you and circle them. These exercises will comprise your Personal Growth Plan.

---

[22] Harry Emerson Fosdick, *The Meaning of Service* (New York: Association Press, 1920), 5.

Faithful Practices of Discipleship: A Personal Assessment

Worship Regularly	Mostly Yes	Mostly No
Do I desire and regularly experience intimacy with God?		
Is there an inner assurance that I am saved by God's grace?		
Am I aware of God's power working in my life and respond to the nudges of the Holy Spirit?		
Do I trust that Jesus is the Truth and rely on Him to be my teacher?		
Is my daily life punctuated with praise, thanksgiving and adoration of God?		
Do I regularly sense the power of God?		
Am I continually driven by a desire for greater obedience to God?		
Do I expect to hear from God during the weekly service of worship in my church?		

Pray Daily	Mostly Yes	Mostly No
Am I comfortable with talking to God?		
Do I desire to know God and desire the things God desires?		
Do I believe that my prayers will be answered and can change things, even God's mind?		
Is there an expectation that God will answer my prayers?		
Am I aware of God's presence when I pray?		
Am I comfortable listening for God in silence?		
Do I offer prayers of celebration and thanksgiving as well as prayers of requests?		
Do I make time daily, regardless of my schedule, to devote time to prayer?		

Learn and Apply God's Word	Mostly Yes	Mostly No
Do I have basic knowledge of Jesus' teachings?		
Do I model my life after Jesus?		
Have I found that setting aside time to read the Bible is an important use of my time?		
Have I found the Bible to be relevant to the struggles and demands that confront me each day?		
Can I say that I read the Bible with pleasure and anticipation that God will speak to me?		
Is my understanding of the Jesus of the Bible sufficient to make me want to give my life to Him?		

Do I expect God to be present when reading the Bible and that he will speak to me through my reading?		
Do certain passages of the Bible come to memory throughout the day?		

Participate in a Ministry	Mostly Yes	Mostly No
Do I believe, at heart level, that volunteer service in the church or community is service to Jesus?		
Have I identified my spiritual gifts and understand how to use them in service to others?		
Am I aware that I am unique, precious and useful to the advancement of God's work on earth?		
Am I willing to place the needs of others above my own need for recognition, position and power?		
Can I identify two or three opportunities for ministry in the church that I could do well?		
Am I willing to invest time in the lives of others?		
Have I taken personal responsibility for the effectiveness of the church in fulfilling its mission?		
Am I passionate about becoming Christ-like in service to others?		

Give Financially	Mostly Yes	Mostly No
Do I trust God to provide for me financially?		
Am I willing to set a goal over the next few years to reach the biblical standard of 10% in my giving?		
Do I ensure that my regular giving to the church remains a priority in my monthly financial obligations?		
Would Jesus regard the way I manage money as an honor to Him?		
Am I able to practice generosity to the church even when I disagree with the leadership?		
Do my priorities include advancing the work of the church?		
Have I prayed for guidance in my financial giving to the work of the church?		
Do I experience joy in my financial support of the church?		

My Personal Growth Plan
(Write your personal growth plan here.)

Listening in Community and Developing a Personal Growth Plan

After you have created your Personal Growth Plan, share it with the members of your small group. Ask them to share anything else they may personally have found to be of value in their own growth in that FaithPractice. You are not limited to the Spiritual Fitness Training exercises found in this manual. Feel free to use suggestions from the group for the final content of your Personal Growth Plan. A useful growth plan should be neither too simple nor overly difficult. Write your Personal Growth Plan here and, later, on a large index card that you keep in a visible place.

Closing Prayer

Prayer may be read by the group or one person on behalf of the group.

Heavenly Father, the greatest experience life can offer is that of experiencing your presence and power for our lives. Thank you for these eight weeks we have shared together - for fellowship shared, lessons learned, and direction for spiritual growth received. If today we are defeated or weakened by anything, grant to us the hope that, as we continue on our FaithJourney over the next weeks, we may increasingly discover the certainty of your presence and love that overcomes all. Through Jesus Christ our Lord we pray. Amen.

The Following Six Weeks

Personally: Determine when during your week you will pursue you personal growth plan. Deciding now when and where you will devote the time required of your plan significantly increases the likelihood that you will take the journey.

You may change the time and place later if necessary but determine now when you will begin. When will you regularly experience silence and solitude of at least 30 minutes twice a week? Use this time for quietly reading Scripture and reflecting on what is read. Begin thinking about whom you will share this experience with, following the fourteen-week process. Your sharing need not be an elaborate undertaking. Coffee and thirty to forty minutes of why you engaged in the process, what you did (your Personal Growth Plan), and any experience of spiritual growth including habits or practices changed or begun as a result.

As a Group: When and where will you gather once a week for sixty minutes for continuing study of Scripture and providing support, accountability and prayer for one another?

When You Gather: Each week your group will use two resources provided with this session. For the first 30 minutes, share with the group your responses to the questions on the *Guided Bible Equipping Sheet*. Six are provided in this session. Complete one sheet no more than a few days before meeting with the group. Do not complete all six ahead of time. The second resource, *Reflections along the Journey*, provides you with an opportunity to share with the group your experience with your Personal Growth Plan and faith journey. Do not complete this resource more than a few days before meeting with your group. For the last 30 minutes of your time in small group, each person will share their responses to the questions on this sheet. Feel free to offer comments of insight and support to one another during this sharing. Close the meeting with prayer for one another and remind one another of the date and time for the next meeting.

To Learn More

Hunter, Todd D. *Giving Church Another Chance: Finding New Meaning in Spiritual Practices*. Downers Grove, Illinois: IVP Books, 2010.

Mulholland, Jr., M. Robert. *Invitation to a Journey: A Road Map for Spiritual Formation*. Downers Grove, Illinois: InterVarsity Press, 1993.

Nouwen, Henri. *Spiritual Direction: Wisdom for the Long Walk of Faith*. San Francisco: HarperSanFrancisco, 2006.

Guided Bible Equipping Sheet

Date_____

Discipleship Insight: Disciples Are Assured of Their Salvation by Grace Alone

READ: Titus 3:4-7

But when the goodness and loving kindness of God our Savior appeared, he saved us, not because of any works of righteousness that we had done, but according to his mercy, through the water of rebirth and renewal by the Holy Spirit. This Spirit he poured out on us richly through Jesus Christ our Savior, so that, having been justified by his grace, we might become heirs according to the hope of eternal life. *New Revised Standard Translation*

REFLECT: In these few verses, the good news of our faith is summarized in a highly condensed form. In your own words, what is that good news?

We are told near the end of this passage that we are heirs – that we have been named to receive an inheritance from God. Have you ever been named an heir in an inheritance? If so, how did that change you life (financially, self-esteem, sense of responsibility, priorities, etc.)?

RESPOND: God has named you an heir, specifically that you will have eternal life. Does this knowledge change anything about how you will live now? Explain.

PAUSE & CONSIDER:

Inward changes in our attitude toward God and others will result in changes in our outer behavior. Michael J. Wilkins

Reflections along **The Journey**   Date_____

What specific actions have you taken this past week toward your personal growth plan?

Have you been given a fresh discovery or insight about following Jesus or have you experienced God's presence this week? Share with the group.

Have you experienced blockages or obstacles to spiritual growth along the journey this past week? Share with the group.

How may the group pray for you today?

Volume: 1-02

Guided Bible Equipping Sheet   Date_____

Discipleship Insight: Disciples Learn & Apply God's Word

READ: Philippians 4:8-9

Finally, beloved, whatever is true, whatever is pure, whatever is pleasing, whatever is commendable, if there is any excellence and if there is anything worthy of praise, think about these things. Keep on doing the things that you have learned and received and heard and seen in me, and the God of peace will be with you. *New Revised Standard Translation*

REFLECT: Why do you think it is important to the Apostle Paul, the author of Philippians, that followers of Jesus "think about these things?"

In the second sentence of this passage, Paul offers his own life as a model that followers of Jesus should follow. Name someone of faith whose life you admire and share what you have "learned, received, heard, and seen" in them that has influenced your own walk of faith.

RESPOND: Identify someone in your network of relationships (spouse, children, friends, etc.) whom you have the greatest chance of influencing by the example of your life. How would you behave differently this week if you knew they were watching closely?

PAUSE & CONSIDER:

You cannot pass (your) faith on to others if you are not living it...and you cannot live it if you do not understand it. A paraphrased quote of George Barna

Reflections along **The Journey**

Date_____

What specific actions have you taken this past week toward your personal growth plan?

Have you been given a fresh discovery or insight about following Jesus or have you experienced God's presence this week? Share with the group.

Have you experienced blockages or obstacles to spiritual growth along the journey this past week? Share with the group.

How may the group pray for you today?

Volume: 1-03

Guided Bible Equipping Sheet   Date_____

Discipleship Insight: Disciples Obey God's Commands

READ: Luke 10:25-28

Just then a lawyer stood up to test Jesus. "Teacher," he said, "what must I do to inherit eternal life?" He said to him, "What is written in the law? What do you read there?" He answered, "You shall love the Lord your God with all your heart, and with all your soul, and with all your strength, and with all your mind; and your neighbor as yourself." And he said to him, "You have given the right answer; do this, and you will live." *New Revised Standard Translation*

REFLECT: Jesus has the lawyer answer his own question. Then Jesus tells the lawyer that he answered correctly. This suggests that the lawyer does not need more information. Something else is missing. What is it?

The lawyer's answer suggests that there is no distinction between loving God and loving your neighbor. What do you think?

RESPOND: What attitude will you change, action you will take, or prayer you will pray this week as you seek to love God and neighbor more deeply?

PAUSE & CONSIDER:

It is not enough just to know (what Jesus teaches); a disciple is devoted to carrying them out consistently and wholeheartedly. A paraphrased quote of George Barna

Reflections along **The Journey**   Date_____

What specific actions have you taken this past week toward your personal growth plan?

Have you been given a fresh discovery or insight about following Jesus or have you experienced God's presence this week? Share with the group.

Have you experienced blockages or obstacles to spiritual growth along the journey this past week? Share with the group.

How may the group pray for you today?

Volume. 1-04

Guided Bible Equipping Sheet

Date _____

Discipleship Insight: Disciples Represent God in the World.

READ: Mark 5:18-19

As Jesus was getting into the boat, the man who had been demon possessed begged to go with him. But Jesus said, "No, go home to your family, and tell them everything the Lord has done for you and how merciful he has been." *New Living Translation*

REFLECT: What insight about following Jesus do you draw from this passage?

How do you think the man felt after hearing Jesus' response?

RESPOND: What insight can you apply to your life this week?

PAUSE & CONSIDER:

Discipleship is not a program. It is not a ministry.
It is a life- long commitment to a lifestyle. George Barna

Reflections along The Journey

Date_____

What specific actions have you taken this past week toward your personal growth plan?

Have you been given a fresh discovery or insight about following Jesus or have you experienced God's presence this week? Share with the group.

Have you experienced blockages or obstacles to spiritual growth along the journey this past week? Share with the group.

How may the group pray for you today?

Volume: 1-05

Guided Bible Equipping Sheet

Date_____

Discipleship Insight: Disciples Serve Other People

READ: Matthew 20:25-28

But Jesus called them to him and said, "You know that the rulers of the Gentiles lord it over them, and their great ones are tyrants over them. It will not be so among you; but whoever wishes to be great among you must be your servant, and whoever wishes to be first among you must be your slave; just as the Son of Man came not to be served but to serve, and to give his life a ransom for many." *New Revised Standard Translation*

REFLECT: Summarize how followers of Jesus are to behave differently than others.

Jesus teaches here that whoever wishes to be great among you must be your servant. Name someone you know, or know of, who exemplifies servanthood in their walk with Christ.

RESPOND: Identify one person who has a need that you can meet this week. What will you do? (Name of person is not necessary)

PAUSE & CONSIDER:

The purpose of discipleship is to help Christians become transformed individuals who imitate Christ daily. George Barna

Reflections along **The Journey**   Date_____

What specific actions have you taken this past week toward your personal growth plan?

Have you been given a fresh discovery or insight about following Jesus or have you experienced God's presence this week? Share with the group.

Have you experienced blockages or obstacles to spiritual growth along the journey this past week? Share with the group.

How may the group pray for you today?

Volume: 1-06

Guided Bible Equipping Sheet

Date_____

Discipleship Insight: Disciples Raise-up Other Disciples for Christ

READ: Matthew 28:19, 20

Go therefore and make disciples of all nations, baptizing them in the name of the Father and of the Son and of the Holy Spirit, and teaching them to obey everything that I have commanded you. And remember, I am with you always, to the end of the age. *New Revised Standard Version*

REFLECT: In your own words, what is Jesus asking his followers to do in these verses?

Why do you suppose Jesus mentions "teaching" after "baptizing" in the process of making disciples of all nations?

RESPOND: How have these verses spoken to you?

PAUSE & CONSIDER:

Discipleship began then, and begins today, as a personal, costly relationship with the Master who came to seek us out.
Michael J. Wilkins

Reflections along **The Journey**   Date_____

What specific actions have you taken this past week toward your personal growth plan?

Have you been given a fresh discovery or insight about following Jesus or have you experienced God's presence this week? Share with the group.

Have you experienced blockages or obstacles to spiritual growth along the journey this past week? Share with the group.

How may the group pray for you today?

CPSIA information can be obtained at www.ICGtesting.com
Printed in the USA
LVOW03s0101051213

363918LV00003B/7/P